RADICAL LOVE

JIM BURNS

D1056345

Regal Books
A Division of Gospel Light
Ventura, California, U.S.A.

Regal Books
A Division of Gospel Light
Ventura, California, U.S.A.
Printed in U.S.A.

Regal Books is a ministry of Gospel Light, an evangelical Christian publisher dedicated to serving the local church. We believe God's vision for Gospel Light is to provide church leaders with biblical, user-friendly materials that will help them evangelize, disciple and minister to children, youth and families.

It is our prayer that this Regal book will help you discover biblical truth for your own life and help you meet the needs of others. May God richly bless you.

For a free catalog of resources from Regal Books/Gospel Light please contact your Christian supplier or call 1-800-4-GOSPEL.

Library of Congress Cataloging-in-Publication Data
Burns, Jim, 1953-
   Radical love / Jim Burns.
      p. cm.
   Previously published: Eugene, Or.: Harvest House Publishers, ©1991.
   Includes bibliographical references.
   ISBN 0-8307-1793-5 (trade paper)
   1. Youth—Sexual behavior. 2. Sex. 3. Sex—Religious aspects—Christianity. I. Title.
   [HQ27.B88 1995]
   306.7'0835—dc20   95-35070
                                                                                        CIP

1 2 3 4 5 6 7 8 9 10 11 12 13 14 15 / 02 01 00 99 98 97 96 95

Rights for publishing this book in other languages are contracted by Gospel Literature International (GLINT). GLINT also provides technical help for the adaptation, translation and publishing of Bible study resources and books in scores of languages worldwide. For further information, contact GLINT, P.O. Box 4060, Ontario, CA 91761-1003, U.S.A., or the publisher.

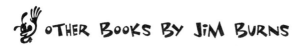 OTHER BOOKS BY JIM BURNS

Books for Youth
Getting in Touch with God (Harvest House)
90 Days Through the New Testament (Gospel Light)
Spirit Wings (Servant Publications)

Books for Youth Workers
High School Ministry, coauthor Mike Yaconelli (Zondervan Publishing)
The Word on Being a Leader, Serving Others and Sharing Your Faith (Gospel Light)
The Word on Helping Friends in Crisis (Gospel Light)
The Word on the Basics of Christianity (Gospel Light)
The Word on the Life of Jesus (Gospel Light)
The Word on Prayer and the Devotional Life (Gospel Light)
The Word on Sex, Drugs and Rock 'n' Roll (Gospel Light)
The Youth Builder (Harvest House)
The Youth Worker Book of Case Studies (Gospel Light)

Books for Parents
Drugproof Your Kids (Regal Books)
When Love Is Not Enough, coauthor Steve Arterburn (Focus on the Family
Publishing)

To
Doug Webster and Doug Fields
friends and coworkers
who by your zeal for life and ministry
challenge me to keep my priorities straight.
Special thanks to
Cathy
for your constant support
and ministry of "lending" me to others.
Donna Gibson Toberty
for your affirmation,
your positive attitude and your typing.
Wayne Rice
for planting the seed
to write on a subject desperately needed
by youth workers in youth ministry and education.
Karen Walters for once again being the glue
that keeps NIYM together.
Thank you for all your extra effort, friendship
and copartnership in ministry.

CONTENTS

Preface 6

How to Use This Book 9

 1. The Story of Tony and Linda 11

 2. How Far Is Too Far? 17

 3. Why Wait? 21

 4. The Sexual Purity Challenge 27

 5. The Influence of Sexuality 31

 6. Sexual Intercourse 37

 7. Differences in the Way Men and Women Respond 43

 8. How to Know if You Are in Love 47

 9. Unconditional Love 53

 10. Peer Pressure 59

 11. Radical Respect 67

 12. Dating 73

 13. Parties 83

 14. Drugs and Drinking 89

 15. Guilt and Forgiveness 95

 16. Options for the Pregnant 101

 17. What About Abortion? 109

 18. Masturbation 115

 19. AIDS 119

 20. Venereal Disease 123

 21. Homosexuality 127

 22. Pornography 131

 23. Sexual Abuse 137

 24. Questions and Answers 145

 25. A Frank Discussion with Parents and Youth Workers 153

Glossary of Terms 157

Notes 161

PREFACE

Three events in recent years have had a huge influence on my life as I approach the topic OF *radical love*. One was a rally in Fresno, California; one was at the foot of our nation's capitol; the other was at a high school in Capistrano, California.

Fresno, California

The night before the Fresno "True Love Waits" rally, I spoke to 350 desperate and frightened but enthusiastic parents about "how to talk to your kids about sex." That night, I asked the adults if, when they were younger, their parents had talked to them about sex from a positive, value-centered perspective. Exactly 12 hands were raised. Most of those parents received absolutely no sex education from home, although a few of them received negative information.

One man said, "On my sixteenth birthday, my mom gave me a set of keys to our car and my dad threw a condom at me and said, 'You'll need this along with the car keys.'"

The next night, more than 2,000 students jammed into an auditorium that supposedly seated 1,400 people. It was a fire marshal's nightmare. I invited the students to make a commitment to a *radical love*. It's a kind of love that goes against the grain of today's culture. When I was finished, I invited them to respond by signing a True Love Waits card and bringing it to the front. I watched students literally run to the front, and when they would see a friend who had made the same courageous decision to wait to have sexual intercourse until marriage, they would hug or "high five" each other. We now had more than 1,500 students crammed into the front of the auditorium, singing and celebrating the huge pile of True Love Waits cards on the steps of the auditorium. The encouragement of seeing those students respond to a *radical love* was wonderful.

A reporter from the Fox television network interviewed me that night and asked, "You mean there are still teenagers who actually are excited about being virgins?"

I said, "Everybody isn't doing it, and some of those students will carry a lot less baggage into their marriages because of their courageous decisions."

I've met thousands of students who have deeply regretted some of the sexually promiscuous decisions in their lives, but I still haven't met a person who chose to wait until marriage and regretted that decision.

Washington, D.C.

The event was "DC '94." In front of our nation's capitol were placed more than 200,000 True Love Waits cards, on which young people had made commitments to *radical love* and sexual purity. That evening, approximately 35,000 people gathered to have a prayer rally and to celebrate the positive decision of almost a quarter of a million students who were standing for a biblical call to sexual purity.

As I walked the Washington Capitol Mall and looked out over the crowd and all those cards, I realized once again that in the midst of a scary culture, a group of young people are making wholesome decisions. That night, I was overwhelmed with the fact that this generation does have hope.

Capistrano Valley High School, Capistrano, California

I stood in front of 24 students in Mr. Leander's first-period psychology class. The topic of discussion was sexual abstinence and AIDS. The students listened attentively and the conversation was excellent. Then I played a game called "To Take a Stand." Basically, I would make a statement, and the students could agree or disagree with the statement; then we would discuss their opinions.

Here was my statement: "It is a wise decision to wait until marriage to have sexual intercourse." They voted. Not one student agreed with that statement. *Zero!* I walked back into my office that day somewhat discouraged, and yet more motivated than ever to offer students the truth that they *can* choose to follow a *radical love.* The cost is high and they will be in the minority of their friends, but this *radical love* of fidelity and Christian commitment will save them from many a heartbreak, and in today's world it may mean the difference between life and death.

The "Straight Scoop"

I was speaking at an all-day event for high school students in North Carolina. It was one of those wonderful times when we were really connecting. I told the crowd of about 2,500 students that the average 16-year-old male has a sexual thought every 20 seconds. They laughed and pointed to all the 16-year-olds who were now ducking under their seats. At the break, a good-looking guy wearing a letterman's jacket came up to me and said, "Hi, Jim. I'm Jack and I'm 16."

I said, "Nice to meet you."

He said, "You know that statistic about every 20 seconds a 16-year-old has a sexual thought? Well, what am I supposed to think about the other 19 seconds? It's always on my mind." We laughed, but he was serious.

Sex and dating are often on the minds of young people (and old people, too!). I believe students deserve the "straight scoop" when it comes to discussing sexuality. During my last 20 years of working with students (Twenty years! I had hair 20 years ago!), I've had the privilege of talking with them about their sexuality, and they've taught me a lot. They've taught me, for instance, that they are mature enough to handle discussing even the most sensitive issues. They have been willing to be open, honest and often quite blunt when they ask questions or offer their opinions. They have also trusted me with accounts of their own experiences and of lessons they learned the hard way. (Because we all can learn from these real-life situations, I've changed my young friends' names and included their stories here.)

Overall, I sense that students today truly desire to be all that God wants them to be. I've met hundreds of Christian and non-Christian young people who are genuinely interested in hearing a Christian perspective on the issues they face every day. I'm afraid, though, that too many students have an incredibly warped idea of God's view of sexuality. I find myself telling them again and again that God is not the great killjoy when it comes to sex. He created sex, He sees it as very good, and because He loves you, He wants the very best for you.

An outgrowth of this dialogue with hundreds of students is this book. Today's young people are receiving all kinds of mixed messages when it comes to their sexuality. The secular world assumes everybody is having sex, and the Christian world—both parents and the church—is often far too quiet. Kids today are making sexual decisions based on:

- Peer influence;
- Emotional involvement that exceeds their maturity level;
- Lack of positive, value-centered sex education.

Studies tell us that the more positive, healthy sex education kids receive, the less promiscuous they will become.

This book is my attempt to give the kids of the '90s the positive, Christian, healthy and blunt material on sexuality they deserve. May this book challenge, inspire and educate you to be all God desires you to be.

JiM BuRNS
Dana Point, California

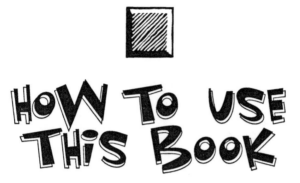

HOW TO USE THIS BOOK

Parent and adolescent or preadolescent discussion: *Radical Love* has been written with the idea that parents and teens or preteens can work through the pages together. Many parents choose to take their kids away for a weekend for "the big talk" on sex. This book was designed with that experience in mind.

Radical Love is much more than a book. It's a learning experience. Although it's a great book to read alone, it's also written with groups in mind. It's based on the idea that students learn best when *they* talk, not just leaders or parents.

Included at the end of each chapter is an excellent experiential, educational curriculum. It consists of three sections. *Things to Think About* provides general questions that will help students clarify the issues presented in the chapter. *Respect Builders* asks students to make personal decisions or take practical action steps that affect the way they view themselves and others. *Team Effort* ties everything together with group exercises and discussion activities that allow teens to talk over their feelings with each other and with trusted adults such as parents and youth workers. This material has been used with literally thousands of students, parents and youth workers, and is now available in one easy-to-teach format. The emphasis is on:

- Discussion and interaction;
- Goal setting and decision making;
- Thinking critically about important issues;
- Relating with peers and adults.

Radical Love is designed for a variety of uses:

- *Small group discussion and interaction*—Youth groups can use *Radical Love* as a helpful and lively interacting tool.

• *Retreat and camp format*—More positive sex education can often take place outside the classroom in a nonthreatening environment.

• *Church school and youth group curriculum*—These subjects and chapters have been time tested to relate to where kids are today. The curriculum is written by Jim Burns—not from an ivory tower, but from a person who works in the trenches with kids.

• *Christian school classes*—This is an excellent resource for classes on health and sex education.

The companion videotape series is also geared toward interaction and making important decisions about sexuality. A companion audiotape is available through NIYM.

THE STORY OF TONY AND LINDA

When I first met Linda, I knew she would be a real asset to our youth group. She was enthusiastic and fun-loving, and when it came to talking seriously about our faith in Christ, she could settle down and really dig in to the Scriptures. What a joy to be around her! Now, two-and-a-half years later, Linda sat in my office and sobbed uncontrollably. Her story went something like this....

Although she had dated in high school, she had never really been serious with anyone until Tony came along. Tony was in the leadership core at church. He was popular at school, active in student government and a real gentleman. At first, most of their dates were double dates or church functions. Very quickly they both fell "head over heels" for each other. For Linda, life began to revolve around Tony and the time they spent together.

A few weeks passed into a few months and the "perfect couple" began to spend more and more time together. After youth group, instead of going to the hamburger stand with the rest of the gang, they would make an excuse and end up spending an hour or so kissing. They both had high moral standards, but they were so much in love that in the next few months they found themselves slipping, in Linda's words, "from light kissing to heavy kissing to light petting to very heavy petting." Slowly but surely their dates had changed from doing fun and active things to situations in which they could be close. Almost every date was filled with very heavy petting.

Sometimes, Tony and Linda would talk about their relationship. Although they were both in high school and wanted to attend college, marriage was a possibility. Now, however, both Linda and Tony felt guilty about their physical relationship. They tried to talk about it, but it was a difficult subject to discuss. Although they both tried to stop being so physical, it was getting harder to stop. They found themselves communicating less and less verbally and more and more sexually.

The Linda who now sat in my office was a serious young woman struggling with guilt and confusion. It was difficult for her to share her experiences. She and Tony had been, in Linda's words, "going all the way" for about two months. The night before, though, Tony had opened up to her and shared his true inner feelings. He loved her, but he felt tremendous guilt about their physical relationship, school was going badly and he wanted to be more involved with church. Although he loved Linda, he thought that the best thing to do was to break up.

Linda was crushed, yet she knew that most of what Tony was saying was true. She came to my office looking for answers. She still wanted to be with Tony, and she desperately wanted to know how to overcome sexual temptation. Linda had found in her Bible a verse that she believed to be true, but she didn't quite know how to apply it. It says: "No temptation has overtaken you that is not common to man. God is faithful, and he will not let you be tempted beyond your strength, but with the temptation will also provide the way of escape, that you may be able to endure it" (1 Cor. 10:13, *RSV*).

Linda believed that God is faithful, and she recognized that her temptation was common to others. Her problem was trying to figure out a way to escape her temptation and remain true to her convictions. We continued to talk for some time and came up with the following:

Six Positive Guidelines for Overcoming Sexual Temptation

Talk About the Problem with Your Girlfriend or Boyfriend
If you don't feel comfortable talking to your boyfriend or girlfriend about your physical relationship, yet you continue to go further than you think is right, then you have a problem. A good relationship includes open communication; in a good relationship the guy and girl should be willing and able to talk about the problem. When Linda finally did talk with Tony, she found out that he had the same guilt feelings she did. Incidentally, talk about your problems while having a soft drink or walking home from school, not right after you've slipped.

Set Standards
The best advice our premarital counselor gave my wife, Cathy, and me was to set standards *before* becoming swept up in the heat of emotions. Set standards that are right for both individuals involved. Again, while having a soft drink, talk about your physical relationship and decide what your limits will be. Then if temptation comes your way, it will be easier not to violate your conscious decisions.

Plan Dates that Will Be Fun and Enjoyable

When Joseph was tempted to lie with Potiphar's wife, he ran out of the house to flee temptation. He didn't even take time to pick up his coat (see Gen. 39:2-15)! One of the best ways to avoid sexual temptation is to stay away from places where it is easy to be tempted. Plan dates that are fun and enjoyable. Double dates, for instance, can often be more fun than "single" dates. Also, in a recent poll of high school students, an overwhelming 92 percent said they would rather go on a "creative cheap date" than on an "expensive romantic date." Plan your dates in advance and keep away from parking spots and dark roads!

Pray Together

As a Christian you will, I hope, desire to be going out with other Christians. A great way to grow in your faith and develop a better relationship with your boyfriend or girlfriend is to pray together. Praying together draws you closer to God and to each other. Praying together helps you set proper priorities for your relationship. And, naturally, praying together as a couple will help both of you resist sexual temptation.

Break Up

One of the hardest things to do is to break off a relationship. We have often become dependent on a dating partner and wonder if anyone else will ever go out with us. There is no easy way to break off a relationship, especially one in which you have been sexually active. Yet, many times the very best thing for both of you would be to break up. If your relationship was "meant to be," you can always get back together later on when you've both become more mature.

Allow God to Be a Part of Your Dating Relationship

People of all ages can struggle to allow God to take an active part in certain areas of their lives. This is certainly true when it comes to sexuality. For some reason, it is difficult to give God this area of life. I think sometimes we're afraid God will be a killjoy.

If it's true (and I think it is) that God cares about every area of our lives, then He definitely cares about our sexuality and wants the best for us. If you, as a Christian, allow God to take an active role in your dating life, you'll find it easier to flee temptation.

Epilogue

Tony and Linda decided to break up. (It wasn't easy!) A year and a half later, both are doing much better. Tony has gone away to college, got involved in a Christian club on campus, and now says he has really pulled his head together. He also says he has been dating a Christian girl who's helping him live up to his Christian standards in his dating life. Linda worked full time after high school and went to a community college at night. Next year, she'll attend a Christian college. She says she has learned to work through a lot of hard times, and she quotes James 4:8 *(RSV)*: "Draw near to God and he will draw near to you." She hasn't dated much in the last year and a half, but is looking forward to some positive experiences at college.

* THINGS TO THINK ABOUT *

- Have you known people who were in a situation similar to Tony and Linda's? How did it work out?
- What do you think Paul means in 1 Corinthians 10:13 when he talks about sexual temptation?
- How do you feel about the suggestion to pray together to help overcome temptation?
- What do you think it means to allow God to become a part of a dating relationship? What are some practical ways in which a couple can include the Lord in their times together?

* RESPECT BUILDERS *

1. Set standards. Have you consciously thought through your standards for dating behavior? If you have, write your standards on a piece of paper. If you haven't, think about it now and write down some of your ideas.
2. Allow God to be part of your dating relationship. How alive is your relationship with God right now? Check yourself on the chart that follows.

ACTION	Never	Once in a while	Once a month	Once a week	Almost every day
I read the Bible.					
I pray.					
I attend worship services.					
I do fun things with other Christians.					
I talk about Jesus with Christian friends.					
I talk about Jesus with friends who don't know Him.					
I ask for God's help rather than trying to handle problems myself.					
I try to include God in my relationship with the opposite sex.					

You cannot keep your dating life separate from the rest of your life. If you are active and growing in your relationship with God, He can help you with your dating relationships. If you come to Him only occasionally or only in an emergency, you are missing out on a lot that He can do for you.

* TEAM EFFORT *

Have one person read the story of Tony and Linda to the group. Discuss the question: What would you have said to Linda if she had come to you with her problem? List several ideas on the board or on a piece of paper.

If you want some help in setting your standards, check the Scriptures listed below. Remember that these are not specific rules. Instead, they are principles you can use as guides in determining what you will do. Write down what these verses teach. Use your own words.

1 Corinthians 3:16
1 Corinthians 6:18-20
1 Corinthians 13:1-7
Ephesians 5:1,2

HOW FAR IS TOO FAR?

I wish I had a dollar for every time I've been asked "How far is too far?" or "Are we allowed to pet?" or "What does the Bible say about petting?" I'd be a rich man! This, of course, is one of the big issues we must face when dealing with our sexuality. Sometimes, I wish the Bible were more explicit when it comes to this subject. But it's not. (Believe me, as a teenager I thumbed through the pages of the Bible looking for answers myself!)

The problem lies, I think, in the fact that most people ask the wrong questions. We shouldn't ask, "How far *can* I go?" Instead the question is, "How far *should* I go?" The issue is not "Am I allowed to pet?" but rather "Should I pet?" People today are often looking for black and white answers. When it comes to the subject of petting, however, answers aren't easy and there seems to be a gray area.

First, let's define petting. Petting is touching, caressing or fondling intimate parts of another person's body. There is no manual that says French kissing is okay but fondling the breasts is not okay. In fact, there is no manual to even say what petting is and what it is not. So for the time being, let's keep it as simple as the definition in this paragraph.

Perhaps a more important question than "What is petting?" is "Why pet?" This is where we might get some real insight. In his book *How Far Can I Go?*, Larry Richards says, "Biologically, petting isn't designed to *satisfy* our emotions, but to *stimulate* and *excite* us, and lead to the fullest expression of sex in marriage" (my italics).[1]

He's right. Petting and arousal (arousal means experiencing sexual excitement) at times can be synonymous. Petting leads toward the ultimate sexual satisfaction—intercourse. Now don't get me wrong. I don't believe that every couple who is into petting will have intercourse. It is important, however, to understand that petting is not designed to satisfy our emotions or our physical desires. Instead, petting is designed to stimulate and excite those emotions and desires.

Something else to think about is that too many times petting is focused simply on personal pleasure and not on the other person. Some people in a heavy petting relationship lose sight of their special friend as they try to stimulate and satisfy their own sexual desires. Petting can become a self-centered experience rather than an effort to communicate love for another person.

The other important thing to mention about petting is the scientific fact that petting is similar to taking certain drugs: It often takes more and more to satisfy. I've spent time with too many couples who have started their physical relationships innocently, but because of the strong drive toward sexual fulfillment in intercourse, they have found themselves guilt-ridden, pregnant or facing a broken relationship. Young people must realize that within every normal human being there is a built-in sex drive. We thank God for it, yet we also must control it. And with God's help we can control it. Who we place in the driver's seat can make all the difference when it comes to our sexual experiences.

Because our sexuality is so important to us, we need to count the cost before we become physically intimate. I think about Janet as I write that sentence. Janet was a lonely girl in my youth group. She started dating one of the popular guys at her school, and, in her words, "fell madly and passionately in love with him." After they broke up, she slipped into my office one day sobbing: "I feel mad. I feel cheap....I have high standards and now I don't even like him!...How could I have given so much of my body to someone I thought I liked but now can't stand?...I sure didn't count the cost!"

That's real insight for a 16-year-old. Unfortunately, Janet learned the hard way and after the fact that her sexuality was personal and that if she gave herself freely before marriage she would probably regret it later. I hope others will not have to go through the pain Janet experienced to learn what she learned.

In this chapter, I've tried not to use scare tactics. All I want to do is give you some facts to think about. Petting is serious business. I'm not writing for the promiscuous teenager, though; I'm writing for the person who is curious about sexuality and yet wants to be all that God wants him or her to be. Having discussed some of the problem areas, now let's look at some of the answers.

Unfortunately, there are no easy answers. Most of the Christian books on youth and sexuality simply say, "Don't pet until marriage." If people followed this advice, they would save themselves a lot of heartache and sorrow. Consider for a moment that the average person falls in love three to five times before marriage.[2] If heavy petting is part of each relationship, there will surely be some confusion as well as pain and guilt when it comes to sexuality.

My answer is not as simple as "don't do it." It is quite possible that you may have a petting experience before marriage. What I want to do, however, is to save you as much grief and confusion as possible. As I said earlier, the Bible is silent on the subject of petting. Throughout the Scriptures, though, we see clearly God's desire that sexual intercourse be saved for your marriage partner. But what about all the other actions, from kissing to fondling sexual organs?

I think an important question to ask is, What would be pleasing to God in our relationship? When we begin to view our relationships with this question in mind, we begin to look at our sexuality from a positive perspective rather than a negative one. For several years, I've given students an exercise in setting standards for themselves. It's an exercise that will help you set standards before you reach Inspiration Point (or whatever you call the local kissing hangout) and find it more difficult to handle your hormones. I've done this exercise with students, and frankly, I'm always amazed at the maturity I see as we consider the question, How far should I go?

It is important to think about this issue and to develop guidelines for a physical relationship even before a relationship develops. Never try to set standards in the midst of passion. Instead, thoughtfully establish the standards for your physical relationship that you feel would best glorify God. Remember that your body is the temple of the Holy Spirit (see 1 Cor. 6:19). Think, too, about what would be best for your relationship with your boyfriend or girlfriend. I think you'll agree in the long run that what is best for God will definitely be best for you.

* THINGS TO THINK ABOUT *

- In your own words, how would you define "petting"?
- Why do people have such a difficult time setting standards for their sexual behavior?
- Do you think guys or girls are more interested in petting? Or do you think both have about the same interest?
- How do you feel about the statement: A person who is petting tends to lose sight of the partner, focusing rather on his or her own pleasure?
- If your boyfriend's or girlfriend's standards are quite a bit different from yours, how will these differences affect your ability to maintain a relationship that is comfortable and healthy for both of you?

* RESPECT BUILDERS *
How Far Should I Go?

Friendship	Dating	Steady	Engagement	Marriage
				SI

L	=	Looking	K	= Strong kissing
h	=	Holding hands	F	= French kissing
H	=	Holding hands constantly	B	= Fondling the breasts
HH	=	Hugging	SO	= Fondling the sexual organs
k	=	Light kissing	SI	= Sexual intercourse

1. Set standards before Inspiration Point. (This Respect Builder goes a step further than number 1 in the first chapter.)

The previous chart gives you an opportunity to think about specific actions and to determine the type of relationship in which each one belongs. Also, consider these actions in light of this question: "What would be pleasing to God?" And remember that God isn't out to make your life miserable.

Before you being to work on the chart, note that the headings range from "Friendship" to "Marriage." At the bottom is a list of abbreviations; each letter stands for a certain action. Write each letter in the column or columns representing the relationship in which you think the action would be pleasing to God. For example, "SI" for "sexual intercourse" has already been placed in the "Marriage" column. We know God's will for intercourse; it is clearly set forth in the Bible. For the other actions listed, thoughtfully and logically determine the standards that will best please and glorify God.

2. If you are in a dating relationship right now, you might want to ask your special friend to complete the chart, too. Then you could compare answers and discuss any differences you find. Just be sure you do this when both of you are calm and rational—not in the heat of emotions!

* TEAM EFFORT *

A debate:

To handle the pros and cons of petting, cluster students into two or more groups of five or six members each. Assign half of the groups to the "pro" side and the other half to the "con" side. Suggest that all students read 1 Corinthians 3:16; 6:9-20; and 10:31—11:1 as they formulate their arguments. (Some may find that they disagree with the position assigned to them. In that case, as in a school debate, they should simply come up with the best arguments they can—even if they do not agree with them.) After allowing some time for preparation, let the proponents of each position state their cases. After each group makes an initial statement, allow time for fuller discussion of the issue.

WHY WAIT?

Tracy and Ron made an appointment to see me in my office. Although I barely knew them, I did know they had been dating for some time. They walked into my office, sat down, and got right to the point. Ron started the conversation by saying, "Last week Tracy and I made love for the first time. It brought us even closer together. We love each other a lot. We're planning to get married in a few years and we want to know why we should wait until we're married to have intercourse!"

I asked Tracy what she thought. I think she was a little stunned that Ron had opened up so quickly, but she nodded her head to indicate that she had the same question. Tracy also had a few more reservations about premarital intercourse than Ron did. She explained, "I did feel really close to Ron, but I've been dealing with a lot of guilt since then. And I'm afraid I might get pregnant or something!"

I really liked Ron and Tracy. I appreciated their openness and their desire to make the right decision. We talked for two hours, and during those two hours they shared more of their dreams and doubts. Yes they did love each other, but both thought they were too young to seriously consider marriage. The conversation also revealed that Ron was much more interested in having sexual intercourse than Tracy was.

When they left the office, I believed I'd made two new friends. They wanted to see me again, but both of them would be away from our town for a total of six weeks for various reasons. Tracy asked if I would think about why they should wait, write them a letter listing the reasons, and then send copies to both of them to think about and discuss together when they returned. That was a unique request, but I said I would try. We exchanged addresses, hugged each other and said good-bye for six weeks. Here's the letter I wrote to them:

Dear Ron and Tracy:

You are two very special people. I think God has great things in store for both of you. I appreciate your willingness to be all that God desires you to be. Our time together on Friday has really made me do some heavy thinking and even some extra reading on what you called "the big dilemma."

Let me preface what I'm going to say by reminding you of what I said Friday. I realize that many well-meaning people make the mistake of "going all the way" before marriage. Although the Bible is clear on the subject of intercourse outside of marriage, God is merciful and patient and He loves us unconditionally. I can also understand how the normal sex drives of two healthy people who love each other can cause an intense desire for sexual union. However, I'm even more convinced than before that it is God's desire for people to refrain from premarital intercourse and that obeying His instructions in this matter will be the very best for a relationship.

I came across this quote this past weekend. It's from *The Screwtape Letters* by C. S. Lewis: "The truth is that whenever a man lies with a woman, there, whether they like it or not, a transcendental relation is set up between them which must either be eternally enjoyed or eternally endured."[1] I can't think of anything more intimate or personal than sharing each other's bodies, emotions and spirits in sexual union. That's why I'm so concerned about today's promiscuous sex. It's the philosophy of "easy come, easy go" or "if it feels good, do it." I know you agree with me that sex greatly cheapens intimacy. I know that this is not the situation in your case. You two love each other and are relatively committed to one another.

I've made up some questions that I hope you will discuss together. They may help you thoughtfully and carefully arrive at a decision to wait or not to wait. Keep in mind that I write these questions with the sense that you are both Christians who truly desire to grow in your Christian faith.

1. Will premarital intercourse lessen the meaning of intercourse in marriage for either of you? (Notice that in all these questions I'll include both of you in the decision-making process. I believe strongly that *both* of you must agree to this sexually active relationship. Otherwise the relationship will eventually be torn apart by bitterness and resentment.)

2. Does your conscience make you feel uneasy during or after sexual intercourse? Could this be the Holy Spirit challenging you?

3. Are you both equally committed to each other?

4. Are you totally convinced in your hearts that the other person is "the one" forever?

5. What do you believe the Bible has to say about premarital sexual intercourse? Here are a few verses to look at: Acts 15:20; 1 Corinthians 6:13,18-20; Ephesians 5:3; 1 Thessalonians 4:1-8; and 1 Peter 2:11.

6. You both seem to desire God's best for you. Will having sexual intercourse affect your usefulness to God or your relationship with Him?

7. Will having sexual intercourse before marriage damage in any way your relationship with each other?

8. Could premarital intercourse damage your communication or result in either a loss of respect for or mistrust of each other?

9. Will premarital intercourse help, hinder or not affect your spiritual relationship to each other?

10. Have you thought through the possibilities of parenthood and marriage because of pregnancy, and using birth control methods?

11. What are your motives for having sexual intercourse? Are they pure?

I'm convinced that any couple contemplating premarital intercourse should take a look at these questions and deal with them honestly.

I also want to include a list of statements for you to ponder. I found this list in an excellent book called *Sex, Love, or Infatuation: How Can I Really Know?* by Ray Short. In the chapter "To Be or Not to Be a Virgin," Ray writes that "science has established nine facts concerning the probable effect of premarital sex on your marriage."[2] I will list them for you. I wish I could include the whole chapter, but I'll simply list the statements. When you get together, you can discuss them as a couple. Don't be afraid to disagree with Ray or with each other. This will be a good exercise in communication and a great chance to learn a lot about premarital intercourse.

Fact 1: Premarital sex tends to break up couples.

Fact 2: Many men do not want to marry a woman who has had intercourse with someone else.

Fact 3: Those who have premarital sex tend to have less happy marriages.

Fact 4: Those who have premarital sex are more likely to have their marriage end in divorce.

Fact 5: Persons and couples who have had premarital sex are more likely to have extramarital affairs as well.

Fact 6: Having premarital sex may fool you into marrying a person who is not right for you.

Fact 7: Persons and couples with premarital sex experience seem to achieve sexual satisfaction sooner after they are married. HOWEVER—

Fact 8: They are likely to be less satisfied overall with their sex life during marriage.

Fact 9: Poor premarital sexual habits can be carried over to spoil sex in marriage.[3]

To be honest, Ron and Tracy, I'm not sure where Ray Short got his information. But I think that each "fact" is worth your discussing. He has really made some important points for you to consider carefully.

The more I think about it, the more I respect you both for taking the time to consider what is best for you, for your relationship to each other and for your relationship with God. I'm afraid too many couples simply move into intercourse too quickly. Without having given it much thought at all, they create a situation that can make a difference for their entire lives.

One last thing before I conclude. Even though right now you have little doubt that you probably will get married and of course don't want to think otherwise, let me play devil's advocate for a moment. Larry Richards says: "One study shows an average of five 'real loves' for kids between ninth grade and the second year of college."[4] You've both said that you have a long way to go before marriage. What if you don't get married? I know that I was thoroughly convinced I was going to marry Geri in junior high, Nancy in tenth grade, and Carol in twelfth grade! It's amazing how our minds can change!

I realize that I've given you a lot to think about. I believe in you both and look forward to spending more time together in the future. Thank you for the real privilege of being included in your lives.

Your brother in Christ,
Jim

* THiNGS To THiNK ABOUT *

- Do you think Ron and Tracy made the right decision to discuss their "big dilemma" with a counselor? Why or why not?
- What stands out in your mind from Jim's letter as being good advice?
- Which of the 11 questions that Jim asked Ron and Tracy were the most significant?
- What did you think of the nine scientific "facts" Jim shared? Do you agree or disagree with them? Why?
- One study has shown that the average person has five "real loves" between ninth grade and the second year of college. Of course, this is a general statement, but how does this statistic affect your opinion of teenage marriages?

Take some time to respond to the questions I asked Tracy and Ron. If your situation is not the same as theirs, answer as you think you would answer if you were in that situation.

- Will premarital intercourse lessen the meaning of intercourse in marriage for either of you?
- Does (or would) your conscience make you feel uneasy during or after sexual intercourse?
- Are you both equally committed to each other?

- Are you totally convinced in your hearts that the other person is "the one" forever?
- What do you believe the Bible has to say about premarital sexual intercourse?

    Here are a few verses to ponder: Acts 15:20; 1 Corinthians 6:13,18-20; Ephesians 5:3; 1 Thessalonians 4:1-8; and 1 Peter 2:11.
- Will having sexual intercourse before marriage damage in any way your relationship with each other?
- Could premarital intercourse damage your communication? Could it cause you to lose respect for your special friend? Could it cause you to mistrust him or her?
- Will premarital intercourse help, hinder or not affect your spiritual relationship with each other?
- Have you thought through the possibilities of parenthood and marriage because of a pregnancy, and using birth control methods?
- What are your motives for having sexual intercourse? Are they pure?

* TEAM EFFORT *

Look at the nine statements quoted from the book *Sex, Love, or Infatuation: How Can I Really Know?* by Ray Short. Discuss with each other what you consider the strongest arguments against premarital sex and why.

THE SEXUAL PURITY CHALLENGE

At age 15, Kim is one of the most beautiful girls I have ever met. Her big blue eyes and radiant smile cause every head in the room to turn toward her. Not only does she possess an outward attractiveness, but her inner beauty shines bright (sorry guys, I'm not giving out her phone number!). One day after I spoke at chapel at her Christian high school on one of my favorite subjects, sex, Kim came right up to me. She had the biggest grin on her face and looked as if she was about to let me in on a secret. Instead, she put her right hand in my face and showed me a beautiful ring. I said, "It's wonderful. Who's the lucky guy?"

She laughed and said, "My dad and God."

I sat down and said, "You'd better explain."

Kim told me a great story: "My dad took me out on my first date. We got all dressed up and went to an extra special restaurant. We had the greatest talk about my remaining a virgin until I am married. He didn't lecture; he didn't preach at me. He just openly and honestly shared his hope for me. When dinner was over he handed me a present. It was a little box, beautifully wrapped. I could tell my dad didn't wrap it by himself! It was this beautiful ring. My dad said, 'Your mom and I want you to have this ring as a commitment to remain sexually pure until marriage.' He pointed out three stones. The middle stone represented my commitment to God, the upper stone was for my commitment to my parents, and the bottom stone was for my commitment to my future husband, whoever that will be." Kim continued, "My first date was with my dad on Valentine's Day, but it is one I will never forget and always treasure in my heart."

After that date, Kim's dad asked if she was willing to pray with him to ask God to help her remain sexually pure until marriage. Kim said she was willing, and they prayed. By this time in the conversation I had tears in my eyes. Kim's goal is to give her ring to her husband on their wedding night.

You may have a special experience with one of your parents such as Kim had with her dad (I hope you do), but the odds are probably against it. However, that doesn't mean you can't take the sexual purity challenge. Here it is: Are you willing to say to God, "I commit my sexuality to you and will refrain from sexual intercourse until marriage"?

To be honest, statistics tell us that you will be in the minority if you take that challenge. Unfortunately, a majority of people in the United States will have had sex before they reach 19 years old. However, a commitment to sexual purity will be one of the most important decisions of your life. Here's what the Bible says:

> Do you not know that your body is a temple of the Holy Spirit, who is in you, whom you have received from God? You are not your own; you were bought at a price. Therefore honor God with you body (1 Cor. 6:19,20).

Because, as a Christian, your body is the temple of the Holy Spirit and because Christ died on a cross for you, you have every reason to honor God with your body. That means, in part, giving God your sexual purity. I have never met a man or woman who waited until marriage who regretted it. But I've met hundreds of men and women who *wish* they had waited because of the "baggage" they have carried into their marriages.

My hope is that you will not wait another moment, but put down this book and take the sexual purity challenge. Right now, make a commitment to God to remain sexually pure until marriage by refraining from sexual intercourse until your wedding night. You won't regret this decision!

What If I've Already Blown It?

Many people reading this book have already missed the mark and at one time or another have been sexually active. They've jumped the gun and are no longer virgins. Here's the good news: You can become a virgin again in the sight of God. Once you have asked for God's forgiveness and made a commitment to sexual purity, it is as if you've never sinned. The Lord told Isaiah, "I, even I, am he who blots out your transgressions, for my own sake, and remembers your sins no more" (Isa. 43:25). That's good news for those who fall short!

In today's world, we need every possible plan to remain sexually pure. A commitment to give God your body and honor Him and your future spouse with virginity is one of the highest forms of commitment.

* THINGS TO THINK ABOUT *

- What holds people back from taking the sexual purity challenge?

- Who can you talk to openly and honestly about sexual issues?
- Read 1 Corinthians 6:19,20. How does verse 19 relate to the issue of sexual purity?
- Why is it sometimes difficult to believe that God actually does "blot out" confessed sin?
- After reading this chapter, what decision(s) have you made about your sexuality?

* RESPECT BUILDERS *

1. Make a decision today to take the sexual purity challenge. Take a moment to pray to God and commit your sexuality to Him. Pray for:

    a. strength to overcome temptation;
    b. wisdom on dating relationships;
    c. your future husband or wife;
    d. a continued desire to remain sexually pure.

2. Tell your parents or a friend about your decision to remain sexually pure. Once you've made a decision, there is absolutely nothing better than telling someone and asking that person to help you remain accountable to your commitment.

* TEAM EFFORT *

Here's a very special, personal letter from Dr. James Dobson to a 15-year-old named Jonathan. Jonathan and his dad had an evening out much like Kim and her dad had. At dinner, Jonathan's dad presented him with this letter from Dr. Dobson:

Dear Jonathan,

Your dad told me that the two of you are about to have a very important talk. I've been invited to participate in the discussion by way of a letter. I was asked to say a few things about purity—sexual purity—though I don't suppose there's much I can tell you that you haven't heard before.

I'm sure your parents have taught you well. But I want to encourage you to act on what you already know. Believe me, it's worth it to save sex for marriage and keep yourself pure for the woman God wants you to spend your life with. The Lord designed it that way for good reasons. Plenty of people who disregarded His plan in that area will tell you how much they regret it.

You're going to need more of this kind of encouragement in the days to come. It's one thing to know what's right. Living by it is something else. Over the next few years, you'll probably face pressure to change or compromise your values—pressure from your friends, from advertising, television and movies, and a hundred other sources. You may even find yourself in situations where it could be easy to yield to sexual temptation.

One of the best ways of fighting back is learning to like yourself. If you feel good about you, you'll have the confidence to take a stand—even if you're the only one! Just remember who you are and what your parents have taught you. There's real strength in knowing that God loves you and has a purpose for you life!

But if you feel inferior to others, it will be that much easier to let them press you into their mold. Don't do it! The rest of your life is ahead of you, and it's worth fighting for. I hope this helps, Jonathan. I'm sure your dad will have more to say on this subject. You're a lucky guy to have parents who care about you so much! Take advantage of their wisdom and be encouraged by their love. God bless you!"[1]

Answer these questions:
1. What advice from this letter is the best advice for you?
2. If you could write a letter to yourself, what would you say to help keep you sexually pure?

THE INFLUENCE OF SEXUALITY

One of the most powerful words in our language is that famous three-letter word "sex." Watch the next time you're with friends or at school. When the subject turns to sex, everyone stops to listen! One of the important questions everyone should consider is why sex has such an influence on our lives. A young friend of mine once made this comment about his own conversations: "With most of my friends, every subject we talk about gets turned into a talk about sex! Our society is sex crazy!"

Well, my high school friend was right. Our society is a little "sex crazy." I saw a T-shirt the other day that had printed in big red letters across the front, "Candy is dandy, but sex won't rot your teeth!" That's probably a true statement, but I think there is more to the whole issue than that! And to better understand our sexuality, it's important to ask ourselves why sex does have such an important influence on our lives.

The Media Appeals to Our Sexuality

Have you ever stopped to realize how frequently and effectively the media uses our sexuality to sell us products? Often you'll see a commercial on television where the most beautiful girl in the world is selling shaving cream. Or Mr. World Universe with rippling muscles, wavy blond hair, a deep voice and a golden tan tries to convince you that you, too, can look like he does if you would simply wear a certain cologne. And what's worse is that millions of us buy that brand of shaving cream or cologne because we fall for this media hype! (Believe me, it doesn't work. I've bought all that stuff and I'm still short and bald!) We are surrounded by sensual media, ranging from billboards to the latest love story at the theaters. And we have to face the fact that the media will always use the power of sexuality to get our attention.

Sex Is Mysterious

Another reason sex has such influence is that it's mysterious. I've been married more than 12 years and sex is still a mystery! I'm not sure there is a more profound mystery in the world. Every healthy person is curious about sex, and that's okay. When I speak at conferences and give the "sex talks," I'm always amazed at what a quiet and attentive audience I have. Is it because of my ability to communicate? I wish it were! It's because everyone is curious. Somehow we know there is beauty in the mystery of our sexuality. I think God made sex mysterious because He wanted us to keep it special. When sex quits being a mystery to you, that is the time to worry.

Sex Is Fun

Now this reason for sex being an influence in our lives might sound strange, but hear me out. Sex is fun. I can tell you from more than 12 years experience that sex is fun. God created sex to be enjoyable. I believe it gives Him great pleasure to provide His children with enjoyable experiences—and let's face it, sex is one of the all-time great experiences! Before you put the book down read on....

One reason people talk about sex so much is that it can be a wonderful experience. Don't be fooled, however, into thinking that all sex is fun. God wants the best for you, and that is why He asks you to save yourself for your marriage partner. And because premarital sexual intercourse is not what God intended for us, it often becomes anything but fun. I've met guys and girls who have had some negative sexual experiences and will bear the scars for their entire lives. Later, I'll talk about sex outside of marriage. The main point I want to get across here is simply that we must be aware that sex is a major influence on our thinking.

No one will disagree that sex has an influence on our lives, but now it is important for us to take a serious look at another important question: How does God view sex? Most of you reading this book believe in God, most of you want to please Him and most of you honestly want to live according to His will. To find out how God views sex and what His will is, we need to find out what the Bible says.

Many Christians need to erase certain ideas of what they think the Bible says about sex because, unfortunately, many of us were simply taught wrong! Well-meaning teachers communicated either directly or indirectly that sex is dirty, rotten and ugly and that we should save this dirty, rotten and ugly experience for marriage. Please get this straight right now: God doesn't view your sexuality as dirty, rotten or ugly!

God created your sexuality. Look at Genesis 2:18-25. It's the story of God creating Eve as a partner for Adam. Adam is ecstatic because the only companions he had before Eve were "all the beasts of the field and all the birds of the air" (v. 19). They may be great for pets, but they're not exactly what Adam had in mind for a lifelong partner. When Adam woke up from his little nap and met Eve for the first time, he was excited. As the Bible describes their relationship, it offers us a lesson: "Therefore a man leaves his father and his mother and cleaves to his wife, *and they become one flesh. And the man and his wife were both naked, and were not ashamed*" (Gen. 2:24,25, *RSV*, italics added for emphasis).

God created man and woman. He created their bodies, minds and spirits. His hand was involved in *every* aspect of their being, and their sexuality was a big part of their being. Notice that when God created light, darkness, the earth, vegetation, stars, birds, fish and animals, "God saw that it was good" (Gen. 1:25, *RSV*). Yet, when God made a partner for Adam, "it was *very* good" (Gen. 1:31, *RSV*, italics added).

In my opinion, any view other than the belief that God created sexuality and that He sees it as *very* good is a warped view. The problem with our society's attitude toward sex is that it is incomplete. Because our sexuality was created by God, we should view it as His special gift to us.

Let's look at another passage from the Bible, this time from the New Testament:

> Flee from sexual immorality. All other sins a man commits are outside his body, but he who sins sexually sins against his own body. Do you not know that your body is a temple of the Holy Spirit, who is in you, whom you have received from God? You are not your own; you were bought at a price. Therefore honor God with your body (1 Cor. 6:18-20).

When I read this section of God's Word, a couple of points really jump off the page. First, our bodies are temples of God. The Holy Spirit of God actually dwells within our bodies. I take this to mean that our bodies are special and that we should treat them with respect and honor. This is true as we deal with our sexuality, decide how much we eat, or work on keeping our "temples" in shape physically.

The other point that jumps out of this passage is that we are to glorify God with our bodies. What you do with your body is one of the few things in life that is almost totally under your own control. You must choose whether to honor God or to dishonor Him with your body. A decision you make about sexual relations may or may not honor your Lord.

Let's face it. Throughout our entire lives—even during old age—sex will influence us. The big question for you and me is *how* it will influence us. Make sure that you question the media's influence. Make sure that you learn what God's desire for your sexuality is all about. Then you'll never have to settle for a counterfeit love.

* THiNGS To THiNK ABoUT *

- The media is mentioned as a major influence on our thinking about sex. Do you agree or disagree? Why?

- What are specific ways to keep the strong sexual influence of the media out of our lives?
- If God created sex and sees it as very good, why would He ask us to wait until marriage to have sexual intercourse?
- Why do you think the world is so interested in sex?

* RESPECT BUILDERS *

1. The influence of sex in the media: For the next few days be especially alert to the ads you see on television and in newspapers and magazines.
   - How many ads use sexuality in some way to promote their products?
   - How many ads use women's bodies in some way?
   - How many ads use men's bodies in some way?
   - How many ads use both men's and women's bodies?
   - How many ads suggest a sexual relationship between a man and a woman?

   Sexuality is also found in the world of entertainment:
   - Think about the last movie you saw—chances are that sex entered into the action, if not the plot! What message about relationships or sexuality did that movie communicate?
   - Was that message healthy or unhealthy? Was it pleasing to God or not?
   - Consider, too, the television programs that are popular. Choose one series and jot down two or three points it teaches about sexuality.

   An awareness of the nature of these teachers—the advertising, movie and television industries—can help us not to be influenced by their messages, which often run counter to the teachings of the Bible.

2. During the next week, keep track of the various attitudes toward sex you hear and see acted out in the world around you. Write down the source and a brief description of each attitude. A couple of examples will start you off.

THE SOURCE	THE ATTITUDE
TV commercial	Sex sells a product.
Guys in the locker room	Sex is a conquest to brag about.

* TEAM EFFORT *

God created sex!

Here's an excellent group discussion starter:
- Does the statement "God created sex" challenge any of your ideas about sex?
- Have you somewhere picked up the idea that sex is dirty?

- Ask God to help you see sex as His gift to you—a gift He wants you to save for marriage.
- Read the following Scripture references and in you own words summarize what they tell you about a biblical attitude toward sex.

WORDS OF THE SCRIPTURE	MY WORDS
Genesis 2:20-25	
Proverbs 5:18,19	
Proverbs 18:22	
Song of Songs 5:10-16	
Song of Songs 7:1-9	
1 Corinthians 6:18-20	
1 Corinthians 7:3	
Hebrews 13:4	

SEXUAL INTERCOURSE

People have described intercourse as "thrilling, soul-stirring, boring, shocking, deeply satisfying, painful, wonderfully comfortable, disappointing, fascinating, disgusting, delightful"[1]—and the list could go on and on. That's why, when teenagers were asked the question, "What subjects do you wish you knew more about?" in a survey about sexuality, the number one answer was sexual intercourse.[2]

This same survey also tells us that nearly 6 out of 10 16- to 18-year-olds have had sexual intercourse.[3] This means that not only are people wanting information about sexual intercourse *before* they experience it, but that they are also interested *after* they've experienced it. We can conclude, too, that people may have sexual intercourse without understanding it. I think it is healthy to want to learn about and to wonder about sexual intercourse. Wondering what it would be like with your husband or wife is definitely not nasty. In fact, it is very normal.

Wondering about sexual intercourse can lead us to want to know what God says about it. We may find that the Bible isn't filled with as many "do's and don'ts" as we sometimes think. The Bible clearly states, however, that sexual intercourse outside of marriage is not right in God's eyes. You've probably heard the words "adultery" and "fornication." Here is how *Webster's Collegiate Dictionary, Tenth Edition* defines these words. Adultery is "voluntary sexual intercourse between a married man and someone other than his wife or between a married woman and someone other than her husband." Fornication is "consensual sexual intercourse between two persons not married to each other."

As a high school student who had recently become a Christian, I had many questions about sexuality and I was frustrated because at times the Bible didn't seem clear enough. At other times, I questioned why the Bible seemed so old-fashioned in not allowing intercourse before marriage. Is God the great killjoy when it comes to sexuality? Many people reading this book have similar questions. I want to help answer some of these questions by stating four reasons for sexual intercourse in marriage. These four reasons are not necessarily in any order; each one is, however, an important dimension of the role intercourse has in marriage.

The Role of Intercourse in Marriage

Unity: One Flesh

In a mysterious, almost sacred sense, when two people have sexual intercourse they become one flesh. Even the physical act of inserting the penis into the vagina is symbolic of the oneness and unity of the couple. The Bible puts it this way: "Therefore a man leaves his father and his mother and cleaves to his wife, *and they become one flesh*" (Gen. 2:24, *RSV*, italics added). This verse speaks of a real oneness in which a couple is so intimate that each person completely shares the other's nakedness. Interestingly, the next verse in Genesis says, "And the man and his wife were both naked, and were not ashamed" (v. 25, *RSV*). This idea of unity as one flesh is seldom talked about today, yet it is a very special aspect of sexual intercourse.

Communication

Perhaps the deepest form of communication and love is intercourse. I am constantly reminded, during intercourse with my wife, that we are physically expressing and sharing our deepest love for one another. A certain tender feeling during this intimate experience communicates a sense of unconditional love, similar to the sacrificial love God has for humankind. During intercourse, you are communicating the deepest sense of commitment. Intercourse only for selfish pleasure is second-rate at best; it subtly communicates a strong message of disregard for the other person that can be quite hurtful.

Enjoyment

As I said in a previous chapter, sex is fun! In my opinion, there is nothing more enjoyable in all the world than the mutually shared experience of marital sexual intercourse. In a recent counseling session, a 16-year-old girl was talking about her problems. Referring to her first intercourse experience, she said, "I didn't enjoy it at all. It was rushed, I was afraid, and the car was uncomfortable." That is *not* how intercourse was meant to be. Intercourse was meant to be experienced in the relaxed, romantic, leisurely atmosphere of the marriage bed—not in the backseat of a car!

I feel sorry for the Puritans of our country in the late 1600s. Many of them actually believed that the only reason for sexual intercourse was "making babies." They were correct that intercourse can create another life, but it can be so much more than an act of procreation. The pure enjoyment, the intimate communication and the symbolic and physical oneness of married intercourse make it one of the most special gifts God has ever given humankind.

Procreation

Of course, intercourse is God's method of creating a child. It is a miracle designed by God. And I consider it one of His all-time greatest miracles and an all-around wonderful idea! The miracle of a male's sperm making contact with the female's egg at precisely the right time to create life is an incredible occurrence! The beauty of two married people who love each other very much helping God create another life, blood of their blood, flesh of their flesh, is beyond the written or spoken word.

God's special purpose in creating sex was that two married people would produce an offspring from their own lives. It is a tragedy that more than a million *unwanted* pregnancies happen each year. It is a shame that something as wonderful as creating new life is taken lightly by many people in our generation. When two people believe they are mature enough to have sexual intercourse, as husband and wife, they should think through the eventual possibility of raising a child. If they haven't dealt with the issue of parenting, they haven't experienced intercourse as God intended humankind to experience it.

Having explored the Scriptures regarding premarital or extramarital intercourse, I no longer view God as the great killjoy. I understand that when you create something as special and meaningful as the intimacy of sexual intercourse, you are wanting the very best for your creation. God knew that the best sex is shared by a man and a woman who love each other unconditionally and who are committed to making their relationship last a lifetime through marriage. I'm not saying that all sexual intercourse outside of marriage produces only negative feelings. I'd be lying to you if I said that. Instead, I'm saying, why settle for anything less than God's best, when it brings the true fulfillment sexual intercourse was designed to produce?

* THINGS TO THINK ABOUT *

- Do the teenagers you know wish they had more information about sexual intercourse?
- About what other subjects in the area of sexuality do you think teenagers want more information?
- Do you think Jim was right to include "enjoyment" as one of the reasons for sexual intercourse? Why or why not?
- Do you agree or disagree with this statement on procreation: When two people believe they are mature enough to have sexual intercourse, as husband and wife, they should think through the eventual possibility of raising a child. If they haven't dealt with the issue of parenting, they haven't expe-

rienced intercourse as God intended humankind to experience it. Give reasons for your answer.

* RESPECT BUILDERS *

1. This may sound like a difficult assignment! Ask a married adult whom you respect and trust to look at this chapter and give his or her opinions on the content.
2. Think for a few moments about the ideas you have regarding sexual intercourse, where you got these ideas and the reliability of your sources. Make a few notes on the following chart to help you get a clearer picture of how your attitudes have been affected by various influences around you. A couple of examples have been provided to get you started.

AN IDEA ABOUT SEXUAL INTERCOURSE	WHERE I GOT THIS IDEA	RELIABILITY OF THIS SOURCE
Sex is dirty. It's dumb to abstain.	Graffiti Friends	Poor They don't really know any more than I do.

* TEAM EFFORT *

A Bible study on becoming one flesh:
    Jesus quoted the Old Testament when He said:

"Haven't you read,...that at the beginning the Creator 'made them male and female,' and said, 'For this reason a man will leave his father and mother and be united to his wife, and the two will become one flesh'? So they are no longer two, but one. Therefore what God has joined together, let man not separate" (Matt. 19:4-6).

Discuss these questions:

1. How does this Scripture describe the mysterious unity between a man and a woman?
2. How is the actual physical act of intercourse a graphic illustration of being one flesh?
3. How does this Scripture go against the world's popular philosophy of casual sex?
4. Why do you think God created sexual intercourse as the method of creating a child?
5. What other insights can you receive from this powerful passage of Scripture?

For a deeper biblical look at the subject of sexual immorality, you may want to check out the verses listed below. You're familiar with some of them. (Note: Some versions of the Bible use the word "fornication" to translate the Greek word that is common to all these Scriptures. Remember, that word means any sexual intercourse between people who are not married to each other.) What do these verses say about sexual immorality?

1 Corinthians 5:9-11
1 Corinthians 6:12-20
1 Corinthians 7:1-3
Galatians 5:19-21
Ephesians 5:3
Colossians 3:5
1 Thessalonians 4:3

Do you get the feeling that people in the ancient world had as much trouble handling their hormones as people do today?

DIFFERENCES IN THE WAY MEN AND WOMEN RESPOND

"Guys can be such perverts! All my boyfriend ever thinks about is sex. I'm not a prude, but I really want to know if there are guys in this world who think about anything other than sex!" I get a question like this at every seminar I teach on sex. And the answer to this girl's question is yes *and* no. Of course guys think about things other than sex. But most healthy adolescent boys can easily spend a lot of time thinking about sex.

It seems to me that besides the obvious physical differences between male and female human beings, some other significant differences are important to discuss—and the question in the previous paragraph points to one such difference. You can attribute these differences to biology, cultural conditioning or whatever you like, but acknowledging some of these basic differences might help you understand why your special friend acts the way he or she does.

Many experts in the field of sex and dating say that one critical difference between the male and female has to do with the relationship of sex and love. Josh McDowell, a popular Christian speaker, says, "I'm convinced sex is more dominant in the mind of a man and love is more paramount in the mind of a woman."[1] When a couple goes to a romantic movie, often the male thinks "sex" and the female thinks "love." After the first romantic scene, the male is ready to park at Inspiration Point and miss the rest of the movie. The female responds more to the idea of love and the beauty of romance. The female is much more interested in the love story while the male is more interested in a replay of the action—now!

As you can see, like Josh McDowell, I'm convinced that the subject of sex is more often dominant in the minds of guys and love is more dominant in the minds of girls. It's not that girls aren't interested in sex or guys in love, but there is a difference. Perhaps the difference stems from what stimulates (or turns on) a guy and a girl. A guy is usually ready for sex any time, any place, at a moment's notice. A girl, on the other hand, is stimulated by romantic movies, flowers or a slight touch on the shoulder. Guys are stimulated by sight, girls by touch. Of course, I'm speaking in generalities!

Guys can be sexually aroused in a matter of seconds. (I'm serious!) It takes girls longer. I've often compared a male's sex drive to a drum solo by your favorite rock band. The male sex drive is intense. It builds quickly to a climax, explodes with excitement, and then ends as quickly as it started. A woman's sex drive is more like a Bach concerto. It takes a little longer to get going. It builds to a tremendous climax, slowly settles down, and then ends softly. Why do I mention these differences? To help you understand and perhaps think more carefully about your actions when it comes to sexual stimulation.

If, for instance, you girls could only understand what you are doing to us guys with what you wear or don't wear! Remember, a guy is stimulated by sight. Now, I'm not recommending turtleneck sweaters or ankle-length gowns for the beach. I am advising, however, that when you get dressed for a date, remember that what you are wearing can definitely help create a mood and atmosphere for the date.

I'm convinced that most of the time girls just do not think about or even realize what they are doing to guys when they dress in certain ways. I'll never forget a time when 16 of us traveled by houseboat for a week. The first night, several of the girls came into the kitchen to visit us guys as we were playing a game at the table. The girls were wearing long T-shirts and bikini panties—and that was it. No bras, and nothing over the panties. After the girls moved on through the kitchen, the guys went absolutely crazy. Their minds had definitely shifted from concentrating on the game to thoughts about something else!

I decided not to make a big deal of it, but to talk to the girls about what turns guys on. The next day we had a wonderful talk. I'm convinced that those girls simply had not thought that what they were wearing would turn on those guys. When it comes to how a girl dresses or acts around guys, she must continually think through how guys react, especially if she wants to steer clear of trouble.

Guys also need to be careful about what they wear and what they say and do. Girls are attracted by sight, but they are also attracted by touch and talk. Guys need to be careful about what they say to girls. I have a friend who told his girlfriend on the second date that he loved her. The problem was that she believed him! She fell madly and passionately in love with him. When he saw what those powerful three words did to her, he backed down and tried to explain: "I didn't mean 'love'!"

What I'm trying to say is that males and females respond differently when it comes to sexuality. Of course, there are also many similarities in their responses, but one of the smartest things you can do is to be aware of the basic differences. Think through your actions and avoid any position that might cause frustration to others. Once you're sensitive to these differences between men and women, you needn't be threatened by them. You may even be able to see how these differences enrich your relationships with members of the opposite sex.

* THINGS TO THINK ABOUT *

- Do you agree that, in general, guys are more motivated by sex and girls more motivated by love?
- What things do you think girls do or wear that stimulate guys?
- What things do you think guys do or wear that stimulate girls?
- Do you think it is important to understand some of the differences between males and females? Why or why not?

* RESPECT BUILDERS *

1. After reading this chapter, list the observations I shared, and then list your own thoughts about the differences between men and women.

	HOW MEN RESPOND	HOW WOMEN RESPOND
Jim's Observations		
My Observations and Thoughts		

Now list several aspects of the opposite sex that could possibly give you romantic or sexual feelings toward them.

2. Based on the differences between men and women discussed in this chapter, what are some things you might need to do differently in your relationships with members of the opposite sex? Make a list and begin working on it this week.

* TEAM EFFORT *

The following two ideas are great ways to gain a better awareness of the differences between men and women. These ideas can be used separately or they can be used together.

1. Separate into two groups—guys and girls. In your group, brainstorm about the characteristics your ideal boyfriend or girlfriend would possess. Then come together and share your ideas. Discuss any differences or similarities between the two groups.

2. Assemble a panel comprised of the following people: a single male, a single female and a married couple. Have the students ask the panel any questions they have about dating or marriage. To help get discussion started, prepare some questions in advance.

HOW TO KNOW IF YOU ARE IN LOVE

Recently, I watched a group of high school girls on the beach check out a handsome lifeguard. (Who says guys are the only ones who look at the scenery on the beach?) As the lifeguard leisurely walked to the water to cool off, the girls went crazy with excitement! One of the girls making the most noise sighed and exclaimed, "I've never seen such a fox! I think I'm in love!"

I don't think her reaction was unusual—in fact, it was quite normal. I even remember saying very similar words when I was in high school and college. (Not about male lifeguards, of course!) Let's think about the girl's remarks, though. The lifeguard may have been a fox, but I doubt that the girl was really "in love." She was "in infatuation." She was attracted to this young lifeguard on a physical level. Perhaps she even had a fantasy of walking hand in hand with him down the beach at sunset. But was she "in love"? Not at all.

I remember my first crush on a girl. Her name was Geri. She was absolutely beautiful. I was totally convinced that someday we would walk down the aisle together. I think I liked her most because she was a better baseball player than I was, and she was also the only girl in elementary school who would play sports with us guys! I liked her for years. In fact, once in junior high school, I wrote a note to her and signed it: "I love you." From that day on, she hardly ever talked to me! I think I scared her away. Was that love? No, it was infatuation. It was what is sometimes called "puppy love."

Infatuation is a normal part of life. Infatuation involves many of the same emotions and feelings real love does. The major difference between love and infatuation is that real love stands the test of time.

From the moment I met Cathy (the woman who is now my wife) I was attracted to her. In fact, I was infatuated with her. I knew that I loved her, though, when I was still attracted to her after two and a half years of dating. Furthermore, I was *com-*

mitted to her. When I first met her, I never imagined she had the normal human faults everyone else has. I imagined that she and our relationship were perfect. As time went on, I saw otherwise. Neither of us was (or is) perfect. The relationship wasn't perfect, and it wasn't always easy. When even after an argument I still cared deeply for Cathy, I knew then that this was becoming more than infatuation. Real love stands the test of disagreements and of time.

There is no easy way to determine whether you are in love for keeps or not. If you are a teenager, something to think about is a statistic I've already mentioned: It is quite possible that you will "fall in love" about five different times between the ninth grade and your second year of college. As a teenager, you will experience various degrees of love, but the odds are against your marrying your high-school sweetheart and living happily ever after. I'm not saying it doesn't happen. I am saying that the statistical odds are against it happening.

As I said before, there are no simple answers to the important question, "How do I know I'm in love?" I do, however, want to give you a few practical guidelines to help you decide if a particular person might be "the one"!

1. Are You Willing to Give 100 Percent of Yourself to Your Partner?

Do you believe your partner is willing to give 100 percent of himself or herself to you? True love is selfless love. Even when you are tired or have had a bad day, selfless love will enable you to meet the needs of your partner. A selfish love grows old quickly when its own needs are not being met.

2. Do You *Like* the Other Person?

I'll never forget a scene in the movie *Shenandoah*. One young man approached another man to ask for his daughter's hand in marriage. The father asked, "Do you like my daughter?" The young man answered, "I love your daughter." The wise old father said, "I didn't ask you if you loved her. I asked you 'Do you like her?'"

Sometimes people get married even though they don't like the personality or behavior of their partner. Often they think they'll change the other person. This plan is rarely successful. So ask yourself if you like your partner even with his or her faults. And consider, too, whether you could live with his or her faults. And consider, too, whether you could live with those faults forever!

3. Are You Transparent with Each Other?

Is your relationship one in which you can be open and honest with each other? Open communication is one of the major tools in a positive relationship. I've never seen a good relationship that didn't have this element of transparency.

4. Are You and Your Special Friend Too Dependent on Each Other?

There are two kinds of relationships: "I love, therefore I need" and "I need, therefore I love." The second kind can be a real loser in the long run. Many relationships, however, are based on this "I need, therefore I love" idea and these usually end up going down the drain. Either one person ceases to "need" and therefore ceases to "love," or the other person gets tired of this total dependency and eventually leaves.

5. Is Your Love Self-Centered?

When a person is infatuated with someone, that person is often asking, "What's in it for me?" This kind of love involves *getting* rather than *giving*. A self-centered love is not a true love; it is a counterfeit love. Our goal in love should be what the Greeks termed *agape* love. This is a love that has no strings attached. It's the same kind of self-giving, self-sacrificing love God has for you.

6. Do You Have a Mature Love for Jesus Christ?

I believe that a good test of true love is to ask if both people involved can honestly say, "I have a desire to be all that God wants me to be. I am willing to put the Lord Jesus Christ first in my own life and in my friend's life. Our relationship to each other is second to my relationship to Christ." The couples I know who are doing well are those who have a good relationship with God individually and together as a couple. A love that is tied together with the love of God is the strongest kind of love.

I would suggest that you take a good hard look at the kind of love Paul talks about in 1 Corinthians 13. The qualities of love he describes in his "love chapter" can be a measuring stick to help you examine if you really are in love. When reading chapter 13, look especially at the qualities of love in verses 4-7.

> Love is patient, love is kind. It does not envy, it does not boast, it is not proud. It is not rude, it is not self-seeking, it is not easily angered, it keeps no record of wrongs. Love does not delight in evil but rejoices with the truth. It always protects, always trusts, always hopes, always perseveres.

This definition of love Paul offers here can help you honestly evaluate your love for another person.

Love is a uniquely wonderful experience. Unfortunately, the genuine experience of love can be closely imitated by an experience of infatuation. As time passes and presents us with storms to weather and new perspectives on our lives, we can then better distinguish between infatuation and real love. Right now, I think it could be important for you to deal with the questions I present here, study the ideals of love Paul sets forth, and trust God to show you His desire for your special relationship. And, as trite as it sounds, time is on your side.

* THINGS TO THINK ABOUT *

- What are some differences between love and infatuation?
- Do you think most teenagers are experiencing love or infatuation?
- Is infatuation wrong? Why or why not?
- Read 1 Corinthians 13:4-7. What impresses you about these qualities of love?

* RESPECT BUILDERS *

1. Have you ever thought about the qualities you like and dislike in people of the opposite sex? Try it now!

QUALITIES I LIKE	QUALITIES I DISLIKE

Go back and put an *X* by the qualities you dislike so much that you're pretty sure you couldn't live happily with a person who had those qualities. Put an asterisk (*) by the positive qualities you think are most important in a person with whom you would want to share the rest of your life. Now you have a somewhat objective way of evaluating relationships.

If you're dating a person who has none of the qualities you really like and several of the qualities you most dislike, you might want to ask yourself why you're dating him or her. And if you're dating someone who has many of the qualities you like and only a few of the qualities you mildly dislike, congratulations! You've made a good choice!

2. Consider the two kinds of relationships I mentioned in this chapter:

I love, therefore I need, *and*
I need, therefore I love.

Under the headings following, write a sentence expressing your understanding of each kind of relationship. Also jot down some pros and cons for each kind of relationship. Then write in the initials of some people you know whose relationships fit the categories.

	"I love, therefore I need."	"I need, therefore I love."
DEFINITION		
PROS		
CONS		
INITIALS		

* TEAM EFFORT *

God's Word gives a beautiful description of love in 1 Corinthians 13:4-7. Open your Bible to this passage. In the space that follows, write one phrase on each line. Then write in the actions of Jesus, of other biblical characters or of people you know who illustrate these qualities of love. Discuss these qualities as a group. The first two have been done as an example.

DESCRIPTION	ILLUSTRATION
Love is patient.	Jesus taught the disciples even when they were slow to believe His resurrection (see Luke 24:13-27).
Love is kind.	My friend helped me figure out my homework assignment even though she had a lot of her own work to do.

DESCRIPTION	ILLUSTRATION

Close by praying that God will teach you to love your special friend, your family and your other friends with the kind of love Paul describes.

UNCONDITIONAL LOVE

Once upon a time, there was a young girl named Susie. She was a beautiful little girl and had the most wonderful doll collection in the world. Her father traveled all over the world on business, and for nearly 12 years he had brought dolls home to Susie. In her bedroom, she had shelves of dolls from throughout the United States and from every continent on earth. She had dolls that could sing and dance and do just about anything a doll could possibly do.

One day, one of her father's business acquaintances came to visit. During dinner he asked Susie about her wonderful doll collection. After they ate, Susie took him by the hand and showed him these marvelous dolls from all over the world. He was very impressed. After he took the "grand tour" and was introduced to many of the beautiful dolls, he asked Susie, "With all these precious dolls, you must have one that is your favorite. Which one is it?"

Without a moment's hesitation, Susie went over to her old beat-up toy box and started pulling out toys. From the bottom of the box, she pulled out one of the most ragged dolls you have ever seen. Only a few strands of hair were left on its head. The clothing had long since disappeared. The doll was filthy from many years of playing outside with it. One of the buttons for the eyes was hanging down, connected by only a string. Stuffing was coming out at the elbows and knees. Susie handed the doll to the gentleman and said, "This is my favorite."

The man was shocked and asked, "Why this doll, with all these beautiful dolls in your room?"

Susie replied, "If I didn't love this doll, nobody would!"

That simple statement moved the businessman to tears. It was simple yet very profound. The little girl loved her doll unconditionally. She loved the doll not for its beauty or abilities, but simply because it was her very own doll.

In this same way, God loves you unconditionally, not for what you do but for who you are. You are His child. Millions of people in the world miss the simple fact that they are loved unconditionally by God. God accepts you. He believes in you and He wants the best for you.

Sometimes we feel that we don't deserve God's love. Sometimes we can't understand how God could have such patience with us when we continually mess up. Well, listen to this: *God's ways are different from our ways.* He doesn't love you only if you do certain things or live a certain lifestyle. He loves you—period! When people finally understand the depth of God's love, they are free to be all that He wants them to be. Interestingly, people who comprehend this unconditional love have an easier time staying away from the sin that can clog their relationships with God.

A perfect illustration of God's unconditional love is found in the story of the prodigal son, which Jesus told in Luke 15:11-32. The parable opens with a father's younger son asking for his share of his father's property. Receiving half of the estate, the young man then goes to a distant country and proceeds to squander the wealth. Soon finding himself without a penny to his name in a country struck by a famine, the boy returns to his father's home. His father sees him from a distance and runs to greet him with open arms. The son's first words are, "Father, I have sinned against heaven and against you. I am no longer worthy to be called your son" (v. 21). The father's joyful reaction to his son's return, however, is to feast and celebrate because, in this loving father's words, "For this son of mine was dead and is alive again; he was lost and is found" (v. 24).

The son definitely sinned against his father. He wasted his money on "wild living." Yet look at what happened when the son asked to come home as a hired hand! The father realized how the son had sinned, but he took his son back with open arms. The father joyfully celebrated the return of his wayward boy.

The reason this story is so fitting in a book on sex is that many of us have had a little trouble handling our hormones. We've slipped from the biblical standard of sexuality. At times, we've even turned our backs on God and gone our own way. But the good news is that, no matter what we've done or how we've strayed, God waits for us with open arms. He loves all His children and nothing in the world makes Him happier than for one of His children to wise up and come back to Him. Be assured that when we do go to Him, He receives us with a depth of love beyond human comprehension.

Before leaving this topic, let's review a few facts about the unconditional love of God.

God's Unconditional Love

God Loves You Not for What You Do But for Who You Are
Sometimes this concept is difficult to understand, but it is true that you are deeply

loved by God. He created you and He loves His creation. Even if you have turned your back on Him, He is there, like the father in the story of the prodigal son, with open arms and warm acceptance. Remember, too, that the Christian faith is not based on rules and regulations; the Christian faith is based on a relationship between God and you. And remember that God never changes this desire to have a relationship with you, no matter what you do. When a person understands that God's love is not contingent on his or her actions, that person's life can be radically different.

God's Ways Are Different from Our Ways
One of the reasons we have so much trouble accepting God's love is that it is often contrary to what we know on a human level. In life, we must often *earn* acceptance by trying out for the baseball team or getting good grades or measuring up to some standards, either real or imagined. But God's love is there no matter what we do or don't do. God loves the drunk sleeping in the gutter in New York City as much as He loves you, and He loves Billy Graham or Mother Teresa no more than He loves you. God cherishes each one of His creations.

God Loves You Sacrificially
God's deep and piercing love for you cost Him the life of His only Son. The ultimate sacrifice of Jesus dying on the cross so that you might have abundant life on earth and eternal life afterward is the greatest demonstration of love the world has ever known. The apostle Paul put it this way: "But God demonstrates his own love for us in this: While we were still sinners, Christ died for us" (Rom. 5:8).

The Gift of God's Love Is Free
All you have to do is accept God's gift of love. One of the hardest things in life is to accept love we feel we don't deserve, but when we do, we can't help but be transformed by God's unconditional and overflowing love for us. As we begin to realize that we are loved despite our mistakes, this deep love will draw us even closer to God.

* THINGS TO THINK ABOUT *

- How did you react to the story of Susie and her doll collection?
- Why do you think people have such a difficult time accepting God's unconditional love?
- Can you relate to the story of the prodigal son mentioned in this chapter? If so, how?
- Do you think it was important to include a chapter on unconditional love in this book? Why or why not?

* RESPECT BUILDERS *

1. God loves you not for what you do but for who you are. Isn't that an amazing statement? Many of us are conditioned to receive love only if we're "good": "Mom won't love you if you keep hitting your sister" or "God won't love you if you sin." When you have that system of thinking, you can change your behavior to receive love. But God turns this around: He loves you, and as you receive that love He enables you to change your behavior.

   Check the following Scripture references and fill in the appropriate columns of the chart. It's okay if you have to leave some of the columns blank for some of the verses.

	BECAUSE GOD...	HE...	WE RESPOND BY...
John 3:16	loved the world	gave His Son	believing in Him
John 3:17,18			
1 John 3:16			
1 John 4:7-12			
1 John 4:19-21			

2. The gift of God's unconditional love is free. Note the word "gift" in the following verse: "The gift of God is eternal life in Christ Jesus our Lord" (Rom. 6:23). We don't earn it, deserve it or buy it. All we can do is receive it.

   If you have not yet entered into a relationship with God by accepting His gift of love, please give it serious consideration right now. It's the most important decision you will ever make. And the step is a simple one. You need only to acknowledge Him with words like these: "Dear God, thank You for loving me. Thank You for loving me so much that You sent Your Son to die for me and to save me from eternal punishment for my sins. Thank You for offering me the gift of eternal life instead."

   If you have accepted that gift of eternal life—rejoice! And think of a way to thank God for it and share it with someone who does not have it.

* TEAM EFFORT *

God's ways are different from our ways. Isaiah affirms this statement. Look up Isaiah 55:8,9 and rewrite the verses in your own words. Or if you're more of a picture person than a word person, draw a sketch or cartoon to illustrate the verses.

Now think of some specific instances that show how God's ways are different from human ways. List some differences in the following chart. I've started the list for you. Share this with your family or group.

GOD'S WAYS	HUMAN WAYS
God wants us to save sexual intercourse for marriage.	Today, people don't wait. Many people also have sexual relations outside of their marriages.
God calls us to love our enemies.	
Jesus gives us the commandment to love our neighbor as ourselves.	
We are to live as servants.	

Here's another Bible story to help you understand God's unconditional love a little better:

In talking about God's unconditional love, I referred to the story Jesus told about the son who left home. Let's take another look at that story. Review that part of the chapter or read Luke 15:11-24, and then follow the instructions below.

List everything the younger son and the father did.

YOUNGER SON	FATHER

Use an exclamation point (!) to mark the actions of the father that show his unconditional love for his son.

Jesus told this story and two others to show God's response to sinners who repent. Read the other two stories in Luke 15:1-10. Taken together, what do these three stories tell you about God the Father and His response to sinful human beings?

PEER PRESSURE

No one is exempt from peer pressure. This demand to conform to a particular group or to society in general is made on people of all ages. The pressure to conform comes in various shapes and sizes. Sometimes it is subtle; sometimes it is blatant. No one having a heartbeat, though, can say that he or she has never had to battle peer pressure.

Peer pressure can often be a spiritual dilemma involving the battle between the spirit and the flesh (the sinful nature in all of us). If you for one moment think you are the only one fighting this battle, you are wrong. Even the apostle Paul suffered deeply from this war within. Listen to him talk about his struggle:

> I do not understand what I do. For what I want to do I do not do, but what I hate I do. I know that nothing good lives in me, that is, in my sinful nature. For I have the desire to do what is good, but I cannot carry it out. For what I do is not the good I want to do; no, the evil I do not want to do—this I keep on doing. Now if I do what I do not want to do, it is no longer I who do it, but it is sin living in me that does it (Rom. 7:15,18-20).

I think Paul was a lot like you and me. He made mistakes and he often missed the mark, but by no means was he an evil person. His deepest desire was to do right. He didn't want to settle for second best, but at times he blew it. His insight about his failings was brilliant. He was able to see this problem for what it actually was— *a spiritual battle*. He really did want to do right, yet he kept messing up. At the end of his little discourse, he answered his own question: "Who will rescue me from this body of death? Thanks be to God—through Christ Jesus our Lord!" (vv. 24,25). For Paul, the solution to the problem of being pressured to conform to the world's standards came from Jesus Christ. Paul didn't spiritualize the issue and tell his readers that his problems were finished forever. He simply knew *who* would help him in the battle.

You can be assured that temptations will come and go, but like Paul, you can be confident that God will help you work through the temptations when you seek His help. Paul wrote to a group of people in the city of Corinth and said:

> No temptation has seized you except what is common to man. And God is faithful; he will not let you be tempted beyond what you can bear. But when you are tempted, he will also provide a way out so that you can stand up under it (1 Cor. 10:13).

In Christ, you have the power to deal with peer pressure. Here are a few suggestions that can make the battle a little easier.

Suggestions to Ease the Battle

Don't Let Peer Pressure Sneak Up on You

Use your head! Know when you are being pressured to conform to a standard that is second best! Face the pressure and carefully think about the possible outcome of your action. Ask questions such as these: "Am I settling for second best?" "Will my actions be pleasing to God?" "Am I being pressured to do something that I feel isn't right?" Sometimes by thinking logically and looking at all the options, we can find it easier to overcome a temptation.

Remember that Everyone You Spend Time with Has an Influence on You

It always fascinates me when I watch groups or cliques of people hanging around with each other. If one person in the group likes a certain kind of music, usually the others will also like that kind of music. If one person wears a certain style of clothes, others in the group will probably wear that same style. Our friends play an important part in determining who we are, what we stand for and where we are going in life. That's why it is important to choose our friends wisely.

God's Word has much to say about friends and companions. Proverbs 22:24,25, for instance, offers us this lesson: "Do not make friends with a hot-tempered man, do not associate with one easily angered, or you may learn his ways and get yourself ensnared." It's all too easy to pick up bad habits from friends. On the other hand, the right kind of friends can influence us toward bettering our lives: "As iron sharpens iron, so one man sharpens another" (27:17).

Perhaps you need to take an inventory of your friends. Ask yourself:

- Are my friends a positive or a negative influence on my life?
- Are my friends helping me to be all that God wants me to be, or are they tearing me down?
- What kind of influence do my friends have on my life?

If your answers show that your friends are a negative influence, it is time to make some major decisions about your friendships. Remember, "He who walks with the wise grows wise, but a companion of fools suffers harm" (13:20).

Choose Your Friends Wisely

I had a friend named Bob. We used to talk for hours. He had a strong desire to do right. He wanted to be a professional baseball player, he wanted to get good grades and he wanted to be a "success with the girls." Bob also had a strong desire to be a growing Christian. He would talk and fantasize about baseball and these other dreams, yet he never seemed to achieve any of his goals. He was always falling down and failing.

Finally, after months of struggling, Bob offered me an insight into his problems when he told me about his "flaky friends" and how they would always bring him down. I said, "You know, it's your choice to be so influenced by those friends. Why don't you spend a little less time with them and a little more time with Robert and Doug?" Bob had told me earlier that Robert and Doug were very good influences on him.

Bob took my advice. He still spent time with his old "flaky" friends, but he began to *choose* to spend more and more time with Robert and Doug. You can guess what happened. Every area of his life began to improve. Because of Robert's and Doug's influence, Bob was motivated to get his act together. Bob couldn't kick the negative influence of peer pressure on his own, but he chose to be influenced by positive peer pressure. And that made all the difference for him.

Remember Your Uniqueness: You Are Special in God's Eyes

Never forget that *God loves you for who you are, not for what you do.* You are a special person in God's eyes. Because of His unconditional love, you are free to be all that He created you to be! Consider, too, that Jesus said, "You will know the truth, and the truth will set you free" (John 8:32). A person who truly understands that he or she is loved by God will not be as motivated to conform to peer pressure. He or she instead understands what it is to be accepted by the One whose acceptance is truly important: God Himself.

Seek First the Kingdom of God

In the midst of our daily activities and responsibilities, it is easy to get distracted. Jesus gave us some sound advice when He said, "But seek first his kingdom and his righteousness, and all these things will be given to you as well" (Matt. 6:33). If we put God first, He will provide the necessities of life. Unfortunately, we often worry more about what people think than about what God wants for us.

An important factor in overcoming the pull of negative peer pressure is the possession of the inner strength that comes from having a healthy self-image. When you put God first in you life, you can develop that stronger self-image. After all, you were created in *His* image! And although you are flawed by sin, He values you so much that He sent Christ to die for you. As you develop this improved self-image, you gain inner strength and then you are better able to say no to peer pressure.

Interestingly enough, the people I know who overcome peer pressure are people who are more concerned about seeking God than they are about pleasing their friends. They are seeking first His kingdom. In fact, as they do that, they seem to have better relationships with their friends than anyone else I know.

It's Hard to Say No

Another topic related to peer pressure and sex and dating is the "it's hard to say no" problem. Many young people have been pressured into experiencing sex when they really didn't want to—simply because they didn't know how to say no. I've talked to a number of people who have really regretted not saying "no thanks" before it was too late.

In his book on teenage sexuality, Aaron Haas reports the results of his survey of teenagers' sexual attitudes. His findings on the subject of "saying no" are enlightening. Teenagers were asked, for instance, "Have there been times when you have been on a date, when you had sexual contact even though you really did not feel like it?" Forty-three percent of the guys who were ages 15 and 16 and a whopping 65 percent of the girls of the same age answered yes. Nearly half of the guys and more than half of the girls who were ages 15 and 16 have had a difficult time saying "No thanks."[1]

What were the reasons these young people gave for acting contrary to their true feelings? Here are some of the answers and circumstances explained to Dr. Haas:

> "I didn't want to hurt his/her feelings."
> "I didn't want him/her to think I was a prude!"
> "I really felt pressured."
> "I just couldn't say 'No!'"
> "I was afraid that he/she wouldn't like me if I said 'No!'"
> "I don't know why, but I felt obligated to go along with him/her."
> "I was high" or "I was drunk!"
> "It meant a lot to him and not much to me."
> "I didn't want to seem like a tease."
> "I was afraid she would think I didn't like her."
> "I wanted to prove I was a man."
> "I did it for the experience."
> "There was nothing else to do."[2]

These statements show that at times people can feel insecure. They can be afraid to say no. They don't want to hurt someone's feelings. I think, however, that any boyfriend or girlfriend who is worth keeping will greatly respect your ability to say "no thanks." If the other person is only interested in your body, then he or she isn't worth keeping. It really is hard to say no, but it's always worth it.

Before concluding this chapter, I want to list a few of the lines guys and girls use on each other. In print they look absurd, but in the heat of passion they seem to make sense. When sexual feelings are running high, even the most honest person may become desperate and try to manipulate another person. Although there is probably a line for every day of the year, I'll mention only a few of the key ideas that seem to be used year after year.

- "It's okay if we both agree to do it."

Usually one person in a relationship is more eager to become sexually involved than the other is. If he or she can get the other person to agree verbally, then that seems to make the action okay.

- "You're the only person I will ever love, so let's not wait until we are married."

This argument is powerful, but usually it simply isn't true. The average person has at least five loves during the teenage years and early 20s. Because this statement about loving one person is usually false, it's a ridiculous line for a person to use—especially if he claims to love the person he's talking to.

- "If you really love me..."

This is the "you've got to prove your love to me" line: "If you really love me, prove it." This line is most successfully used by macho older guys who are dating younger girls. Sometimes a person with a poor self-image falls for this line also.

- "Let's experiment to see what it's like. If we don't like it, we'll never have to do it again."

People actually fall for this! The aggressor knows that if the partner gives approval once, he or she will most likely give in again at other times. Remember that it's harder to say no the second time.

- "Everybody's doing it. Are you a square?"

First let me say, "Wrong! Everybody isn't doing it!" On any junior high, high school or college campus, people have chosen not to be sexually active—and often they are the real leaders in the school. You are not a square if you choose not to engage in sexual promiscuity. You are a square if you succumb to peer pressure because of a flimsy line like this one!

- "If it happens, it happens!"

These words are usually said by the person who is always raising the subject of sex. Be careful of people who are always raising philosophical questions about sex, asking personal questions about your sex life and harping on the subject so much that it would be easy to be tempted. This line is a sly one, but it works—just ask thousands of disappointed girls and guys who fell for it.

Peer pressure is real. It's a fact of life we all must deal with at any age, but the pressure seems much more difficult to deal with at certain times of our lives. I know that peer pressure combined with a poor self-image and a deep love for another person can cause us to do things we might later regret. We can deal with this pressure more easily when we choose friends who will be supportive of us. It also helps to spend time considering God's love for us. Trust in this love and rely on God's promises to be with you as you face temptations and pressure from your peers.

* THINGS TO THINK ABOUT *

- Why is it so difficult to fight the battle of peer pressure?
- Why do you think so many people have such a problem saying no to sex even when they don't want to have it?
- Do you agree or disagree with the idea that the people you spend time with have a profound influence on you? Why?
- What makes you unique in God's eyes?

* RESPECT BUILDERS *

1. Choose your friends wisely. Remember, this doesn't necessarily mean you will totally drop someone who is having a bad influence on you. That person may need the *good* influence for Christ that you can offer to him or her. But you might want to find a better balance of time spent with that person and time spent with people who are good influences.

    Write down the initials of people with whom you spend time. Then use a "+" or a "-" to indicate whether each person is, in general, a good or bad influence. Then determine roughly what percentage of your time is spent with each person, and write the figures in the third column.

THE PEOPLE	THE INFLUENCE	THE TIME

Looking at the chart, what change in the percentages you've written do you think you might need to make?

2. Everyone you spend time with has an influence on you. Scripture has much to say about the way friends can influence us for good or for bad. Read the Scripture references indicated here and summarize what each one says about the good or bad influence of friends.

	A FRIEND'S GOOD INFLUENCE	A FRIEND'S BAD INFLUENCE
Proverbs 13:20		
Proverbs 17:17		
Proverbs 18:24		
Proverbs 22:24,25		
Proverbs 27:17		

Now think seriously about the people with whom you spend the most time.

HOW ARE MY FRIENDS INFLUENCING ME?	HOW AM I INFLUENCING MY FRIENDS?

Look at the way you completed the chart. Do you need to make some changes in the amount of time you spend with certain people or in the way you allow yourself to respond to those people? Be specific—don't answer with just a yes or no!

* TEAM EFFORT *

It's hard to say no:

Sometimes it helps if you think through an answer before you need it. The following statements are some of the most popular "lines" people of both sexes use to try to manipulate another person into sexual activity. Think through each statement and come up with a response. Your responses may be logical, witty or outrageous—whatever you want them to be. Share your responses with the group.

- "It's okay if we both agree to do it."
- "You're the only person I will ever love, so let's not wait until we're married."
- "If you really love me, you will do it."
- "Let's experiment to see what it's like. If we don't like it, we'll never have to do it again."
- "Everybody's doing it! What's wrong with you?"
- "If it happens, it happens!"

Having thought about these "lines," you're probably now better prepared to deal with one if it ever comes your way!

RADICAL RESPECT

Jason and Jennifer were boyfriend and girlfriend. They had been dating for seven months. One day when I was speaking at a "Handling Your Hormones" sexuality event for high school students, I used them as an illustration. I didn't know them before the event, and little did I know that my illustration would affect their relationship forever. I wanted to get the point across that as Christians we are called to "radically respect" our boyfriends or girlfriends. I wanted the crowd to understand that because we are Christians we are to treat each other as if Jesus lived in each believer. Why? Because He actually does (check out 1 Cor. 6:19).

I looked around the room for a couple holding hands. I picked out Jason and Jennifer. I asked, "Have you two been dating?" They nodded yes. I asked their names. Then I said, "Jason, you are not just dating Jennifer, who is very beautiful, has a wonderful personality and is a Christian, but you are dating the Jesus who lives inside Jennifer. Treat her with a radical respect. She is a child of God. And Jennifer (she blushed), you aren't just dating Jason, an outgoing guy, a real hunk and a Christian, but according to the Bible, you are dating the Jesus who lives inside Jason. Jason is a very special child of God. You are to respect him as if Jesus were present in his life."

These two beautiful people just smiled and I went on with my point. However, six months later I got a call from Jason to say thanks. He said that he and Jennifer were about "one week" from going all the way, and they had never thought of treating each other with a radical respect. That very day, they decided to treat each other as God would want, and they did not have sexual intercourse. The apostle Paul's advice to us is to "outdo one another in showing honor" (Rom. 12:10, *RSV*). The Christian approach to dating and relating to the opposite sex must be radically different from what we see in the secular media. We are to treat each other as children of God. Jesus Christ lives with each believer by the power of the Holy Spirit.

Here's an important principle: The radical difference between love and sex is, if you love someone you want the best for him or her. Radical respect means putting the needs of others above our own desires. Jason didn't have sex with Jennifer because he knew it was not best in the long run for Jennifer. He had the intelligence to realize that although they really liked each other, there was a good chance they would not get married. Radical respect means looking out for the other's interest above your own. Here's how Paul described the attitude of Jesus:

> Do nothing out of selfish ambition or vain conceit, but in humility consid-er others better than yourselves. Each of you should look not only to your own interests, but also to the interests of others. Your attitude should be the same as that of Christ Jesus (Phil. 2:3-5).

It's pretty clear—the Christian approach to dating is radically different.

Some people reading this may believe the same as the 18-year-old, sexually active friend of mine who exclaimed, "God is the great killjoy when it comes to sex." I don't think so. Although the Bible is definitely not a sex manual, I believe its words and values clearly have our best interest in view.

What the Bible Says About...

Adultery

> "You shall not commit adultery" (Exod. 20:14).

Adultery is when two people have sexual intercourse and at least one of them is married to someone else. To put it simply, adultery tears lives apart and usually causes an incredible amount of turmoil, not only for the couple, but for the others involved. Cathy and I have friends who have broken up their marriages because of adulterous affairs, and it has *never* been easy. Relationships are broken and pain is the result. When God tells us in the Ten Commandments, "You shall not commit adultery," He surely is not the great killjoy. He simply wants the best for us.

Fornication

> It is God's will that you should be sanctified: that you should avoid sexual immorality (1 Thess. 4:3).

Fornication is when two people have sexual intercourse and neither are married. Again, I believe it's pretty evident that God wants the best for us and that's why He commands us to flee from immorality and fornication. I often have the privi-lege of performing wedding ceremonies of people close to me. In my premarital counseling sessions I always ask the question, "What kind of baggage are you bringing into this relationship?" I'm referring to a dysfunctional family, alcoholism, sexual abuse or other issues of trauma. Almost always the first answer is, "Well, I was in this other relationship, and we went too far physically." Please remember, there are consequences to our sexual actions. It's true God forgives us, but most people who are sexually active before marriage still feel the consequences. The best way to keep from suffering the consequences of a sexual relationship is to take this command from God seriously and obey God's Word. Flee from fornication!

One Flesh

> "Haven't you read,...that at the beginning the Creator 'made them male and female,' and said, 'For this reason a man will leave his father and mother and be united to his wife, and the two will become one flesh'? So they are no longer two, but one. Therefore what God has joined together, let man not separate" (Matt. 19:4-6).

This is a noteworthy quote from the lips of Jesus. When a man and a woman come together sexually, two become one! The very act of intercourse is a perfect illustration of two becoming one. Today, one of the major philosophies being touted is that casual sex is okay. I honestly don't believe in casual sex. How can two people become one and call that "casual"?

The Answer: Radical Respect

> Flee from sexual immorality. All other sins a man commits are outside his body, but he who sins sexually sins against his own body (1 Cor. 6:18).

We are challenged in this passage to flee, or run, from sexual immorality. Verse 18 apparently tells us that sin is sin, but that sexual sin is against our own bodies. When we sin against our bodies, the temples of God, it tends to stay with us longer psychologically and emotionally. Frankly, I know people who made negative sexual decisions in junior high and high school who are now middle-aged and are still dealing with the sexual sins of their teenage years. I'm not talking just about people who got pregnant. I'm talking about people's emotions and feelings being paralyzed because of past experiences.

> Do you not know that your body is a temple of the Holy Spirit, who is in you, whom you have received from God? You are not your own; you were bought at a price. Therefore honor God with your body (1 Cor. 6:19,20).

Because our bodies are the temples of God through the Holy Spirit, we *must* treat each other with the utmost respect. To treat one another as a temple of God means to treat the other person with honor. Jason treated Jennifer with respect because of his commitment to God.

To look at this passage another way, we understand that Jesus Christ gave His body for us on the cross. Now as Christians, our response to the Cross is to give our bodies to God. One of the most important elements of being a follower of Jesus Christ is to honor and obey Him by giving Him your body. Paul put it this way:

> Therefore, I urge you, brothers, in view of God's mercy, to offer your bodies as living sacrifices, holy and pleasing to God—this is your spiritual act of worship (Rom. 12:1).

God doesn't want to kill our joy when it comes to sexuality. He created sex. It's His idea. He wants the best for us, and His challenge to every Christian is that of "radical respect."

* THINGS TO THINK ABOUT *

- Radical respect is definitely a different philosophy from what you hear about in the secular world. What do you see as the differences?
- Our bodies are the temples of the Holy Spirit. How does this principle affect your relationship with people of the opposite sex?
- What are specific, practical ways you can "outdo one another in showing honor" in a dating relationship?
- Do you view the radical respect philosophy as one of many options for Christian dating or the only option for a Christ-centered relationship?

* RESPECT BUILDERS *

1. Watch your language! A great respect builder is to watch how you talk about people of the opposite sex (and the same sex for that matter). When you are talking about a person being "easy" sexually or describing their bodies in sexual terms, you are talking about a child of God, created in His image. Christians are challenged to *love* and *encourage* each other with our lives and with our words. Next time you are ready to make a sexual joke or innuendo, hold your tongue!
2. Treat each person you know as a child of God. Read Matthew 25:34-40. This passage is about meeting the needs of the poor and oppressed. Look at verse 40 and write out how this verse especially relates to the radical respect concept.

* TEAM EFFORT *

Radical respect:

Below are listed several "situations." Write out and then discuss with your group or family how you would apply radical respect to each situation:

- Listening to other students talk in sexual innuendoes to a girl or guy on campus;
- Going farther on a date than you feel is right before God;
- Taking a date to a sexually explicit movie;
- Dating a non-Christian;
- Kissing, fondling breasts, oral sex.

DATING

I can always tell when the high school prom is about to take place. Many of the girls in my youth group begin to feel extremely depressed. It's the Sunday before the big dance and it looks like they'll be spending another prom night at the movies with their girlfriends, who also weren't asked to the prom. To tell you the truth, I'm beginning to resent proms because of all the damage they do to the self-images and emotions of my young friends. It is a shame that an event that draws only about 25 percent of the school's population can do so much damage to so many of those not attending.

This emphasis on the prom brings into focus the fact that the great American institution—the date—is going as strong as ever. For many of us, dating is a great paradox. Most people dream of the perfect romantic date. Most young people can hardly wait to start dating. Dating can be great fun. It can be all you ever dreamed about. But the paradox is that dating can also cause more distress, hurt feelings and self-doubt than just about anything else I've ever seen. Before we deal with some helpful advice, I want to clear up two misunderstandings about dating.

Misunderstanding 1: *Almost everybody dates in high school.*
Wrong. Statistics tell us that 50 percent of the girls and 40 percent of the guys graduating from high school have *never* dated. If you happen to fall into this category, you are definitely not alone. Here's a note from the back of a church bulletin that a youth volunteer gave to me one time after I shared this statistic at a youth meeting: "Thanks, Jim, for letting our kids know that not everyone dates in high school. The biggest problem in my life was that I didn't date in high school. I thought I was the only one. I hated myself, my looks, my personality, my church—everything. Years later, I realized how grateful I was for being a 'late bloomer.' I was able to establish positive high school friendships that have lasted a lifetime, and I have a wonderful husband I met while in college. I wish I'd heard your talk years ago."

Here's an excerpt from another letter that has a different perspective on the same issue: "I wish I hadn't dated at such a young age. I didn't know how to handle my emotions. I let guys use me. Of course I wasn't aware of this at the time. But now, after two abortions, I wish I hadn't grown up so fast."

Misunderstanding 2: *If you want to be popular, you must be sexually active.*
Again, this is simply wrong. *Everybody isn't doing it!* Of the high schoolers who were elected to Who's Who Among American High School Students in 1982, 73 percent had never had sexual relations. If you could survey some of the popular people at your school, you would find out that not everyone is sexually active. Yes, they have a normal sex drive and curiosity and all the rest, but they recognize that they must deal with other more important priorities.

One of the finest compliments I've ever heard was a statement by a young girl in our youth group. She was telling me about one of our high school seniors whom she described in this way: "John is cute, he is popular at school, and he's so involved in sports. I love being around him because he's so together, and if you can believe this, he is still a virgin!"

I think my young friend was amazed that a person could be cute, popular and "together" and still *choose* to be a virgin. Thousands of people have chosen as an act of their wills *not* to be sexually active and still seem to have a lot of friends and a certain degree of popularity.

A few things I've said are worth repeating. First, it isn't true that everybody dates in high school. Second, it isn't necessary to be sexually active to be popular. Dating can be fun—and your time for dating will come. Whether that time is now or in the future, I have some suggestions for you.

Dating Suggestions

Establish a Friendship
As I shared earlier, the first day I saw the woman who is now my wife, I fell deeply "in infatuation" with her. She didn't know I existed, but I knew it was "infatuation at first sight." Back then, I might have said "*love* at first sight," but now I know better. Anyway, I'll never forget that day in the campus gym.

I was at freshman orientation with two other newcomers to the college whom I had met at dinner. Cathy was being entertained by a group of upperclassmen who seemed to have some of the same feelings I had! I leaned over to my two freshman friends, pointed out Cathy to them, and said, "See that girl over there? I'm going to take her out sometime." They looked at her, they looked at me, and they laughed. They thought I was kidding, but I wasn't.

I was lucky enough to have the same English class and psychology class Cathy had. I would try to sit next to her whenever I could manage it—which was pretty often because I would wait for her to come in before I would sit down.

Well, to make a long story short, we became "just friends." Cathy had another boyfriend and she would even tell me about their dates. But you know what? By becoming "just friends" we established a brother/sister relationship that served as a solid foundation between us. We spent a large amount of time talking and becoming closer friends. We had a great deal of fun together long before we became boyfriend and girlfriend.

I think that's why, after knowing each other for almost 20 years, we still like being together. We started off as friends rather than lovers. Far too often, though, people in a dating relationship do not work on establishing a friendship. That's why some relationships develop many hurt feelings and misunderstandings.

Avoid Isolation

Another factor to consider in a dating relationship is to avoid isolating yourself. If you spend time only with your boyfriend or girlfriend and you have little time with your own friends, you probably have a poor relationship.

Often the following imaginary scene happens in real life: Boy and girl meet. They like each other very much. They spend more time with each other. They come to enjoy each other's company so much that they begin to exclude their other friends. Finally, they spend little or no time with anyone else. Their friends complain, but to no avail. Boy and girl become sexually involved. They break up. Both are feeling the heartbreak. Both feel like they've lost their other friends, too, and that they have no one to turn to in their loneliness.

In a positive dating relationship, even when people are "going steady," they must maintain old friendships and spend time with other people. A positive relationship does not involve complete dependency; it involves a mutual love and respect that says, "I love you so much that I'm willing to share you with your friends."

Don't Stay Together Only for Security

One of the most difficult things to do in life is to break off a relationship, yet, often it must be done. Most teenage relationships go on too long to be truly healthy. Then when they end, the emotional trauma cuts deep. Often one or both partners will attempt to restore the relationship. But there is nothing worse than trying to put back together something that should not be put back together. If you are hanging on to a relationship simply for the security it offers, muster up all your courage and break it off. The sooner you break up, the easier it will be.

Sometimes we don't know how to act around a person with whom we have ended a relationship. Try to continue to be friends. It might take time, but try to maintain a friendship. Perhaps it will eventually turn into a closer relationship. To do this, you'll have to stay away from gossiping or telling negative stories about your "ex." Try to put your differences aside and work at developing a brother/sister relationship.

Plan Fun and Enjoyable Dates

The average American date seems to consist of dinner, movie and making out! I'm sure I'm exaggerating—but only a little! Because the purpose of dating is to become better friends, it's important to plan dates that will help you get to know each other better. Many dates are boring because people do the same thing at the same time at the same place. Sameness can cause even a good relationship to go sour, so be creative with your dates.

In case you don't feel creative, here are more than 90 creative and not-so-creative date suggestions. I've compiled these through the years in brainstorming sessions with high schoolers and by reading a couple of helpful books. Read through the list, think of other ideas on your own and be creative with your dating life!

ACTiVE DATES/SPORTS

Ride bikes or a bicycle built for two
Visit a beach or lake
Ice skate
Shop
Play backgammon
Canoe
Go horseback riding
Try hiking or climbing
Dance
Play pinball or miniature golf
Play croquet
Water-ski
Bowl
Try creative writing (poems, short stories)
Take up photography
Visit a batting cage
Play Ping-Pong
Play board games or card games
Take an exercise class together
Plant a garden together
Wash your cars together
Read a book aloud together
Do homework together
Collect something together

Take a walk
Roller-skate
Play tennis
Learn to play racquetball
Sail
Fly kites
Fish
Ride a ferry
Attend a Bible study
Go for a drive
Snow ski
Jog
Get involved in handcrafts (Refinish an old piece of furniture! Experiment with ceramics!)
Take a fun class together (Conversational French, photography, watercolor painting)
Go on a scavenger hunt
Go to the river for rafting or tubing
Play badminton
Build a tree house
Ride motorcycles

FooD

Go out to dinner—casual or fancy
Go home for lunch
  during the school day
Share a pizza and talk
Have a barbecue
Go on a picnic
Cook dinner for your parents

Take an ice-cream
  break and talk
Kidnap the other person
  for breakfast
Cook dinner together
Bake cookies
Make homemade ice cream

SPECTATOR

Attend a play
Go to the movies
Support school functions
Enjoy parties and friends
Go to a sports event
Visit a swap meet, an
  auction or garage sales
Feed the ducks

Watch TV at someone's
  house
Go to a concert
Attend a Bible study
Watch hang gliders
Go to public lecture
Hear a public speaker

PLACES To Go

The mountains
An interesting historical site
The circus
The mountains in winter
  to play in the snow and
  build snowpeople
An observatory
The county fair

The beach
Museums
The zoo
The park and swing
Church and youth
  group functions
The swap meet, an
  auction or garage sales

SERVE OTHERS

Have a Bible study
Work at church together

Do volunteer work
  together

Remember that Dating Is Preparation for Marriage

Not every person you date will be someone you would want to marry, but most of
the people you date will become someone's marriage partner. That's why dating is
good preparation for marriage. I think you should treat each date as a special date.
By dating, you can learn a lot about the kind of person you would like to marry. As
you date a variety of people, you will get a better view of what you want in a mate.

At times it frightens me when two people who have dated only each other plan to get married. Most people need to experience a variety of relationships before they settle down for that one special lifelong relationship. Listen to what a friend of mine told me recently: "I knew I loved Karen, but I never realized how much until one summer in college when we decided to date others. And, you know, that time really helped me see what it was I liked about Karen, and it only convinced me more that I was in love with her."

Another real benefit of dating is that you get a better idea of how you relate to the opposite sex in various situations. It can teach you some important things about yourself and about getting along with another person. And these lessons will help you be more sensitive and act more appropriately when you are ready to settle down and get married.

One last thought before we move on. Because each person you date is created by God and loved by our Lord, you should treat him or her with the same respect, dignity and kindness you want to receive from others. Remember, too, that many of the people you date will become someone else's spouse. And realize that someone may be dating your future spouse right now.

Avoid Getting Too Close Too Soon

My friend Mike Yaconelli recently gave me something to think about. He works with young people and seems to understand what's happening among them today. He said, "Today it seems that too many kids take breaking up with a boyfriend or girlfriend way too hard. Their grief is almost as if they were married and going through a divorce." He then made this crushing statement: "I think it's because too many young people are having sex so soon after they meet that they are dealing with a deeper kind of intimacy than young people were even a few years ago."

You know what? Mike is right. Kids are becoming intimate so soon in their relationships that it is taking a terrible toll on their emotional health. Consider the following scenario.

Tim and Susie like each other. In fact, they think they love each other. They hadn't meant to get so deeply involved physically, but they have. Call it curiosity, lust, sex drive or just enjoying each other's touch. Whatever you call it, now they're in trouble. They've been intimate, but neither one is emotionally able to handle the deep commitment that goes with physical intimacy. The relationship begins to deteriorate until finally they break it off. It's too bad because they might have become a great couple. Instead, they must suffer the painful emotional consequences that come with breaking off physical intimacy.

If you have or would like to have a special relationship, move very slowly. That special friendship is worth the wait and the slower pace could possibly be one of the wisest decisions you will ever make. No one I've ever met who has waited to get physical in a relationship has ever regretted waiting. Think about that statement for a minute. I surely can't say the same about the number of my friends who didn't wait.

Advice on Dating Non-Christians

Now for the big question: Should Christians date non-Christians? Every time I speak at a conference, every time I give a talk related to sex, and any time the subject of dating comes up, I am asked for my opinion on Christians dating non-Christians. Here it is.

Contrary to the belief of some people, all non-Christians are not interested in going to bed on the first date. All non-Christians are not pot smokers or heavy drinkers. I know many fine non-Christians. Some of the kindest, gentlest, most talented people I know do not profess faith in the Lord Jesus Christ. I think it is a shame that well-meaning Christians give us advice that seems to say, "Stay away from non-Christian pagans. They'll only pull you down!" It seems to me that Jesus said something about us Christians being the salt of the earth and the light of the world (see Matt. 5:13,14). Jesus spent time with sinners and helped them understand the real meaning of life. I think, then, that a Christian should be able to name some close non-Christian friends. I hope you are cultivating deep relationships with Christians and non-Christians alike.

I don't, however, believe in what some people call "missionary dating"—that is, dating a non-Christian to make him or her a Christian. Once in a great while this plan works, but most often it leads to hurt, rejection, misunderstanding and at times a real falling away from God. Although I believe we all need to have non-Christian friends, I'm afraid that when a Christian and non-Christian date, it is similar to mixing apples and oranges.

Let me explain: No verses in the Bible say "Thou shalt not date nonbelievers." Clear-cut guidelines, however, tell us we should not *marry* nonbelievers. Guess what? Dating leads to marriage.

I've seen too many relationships end in disaster when one person was a Christian and the other wasn't. I'm sure you've heard the horror stories also. Boy meets girl; they fall in love. Boy falls away from God because his new "god" is his girlfriend. Or boy meets girl and they fall in love. Boy and girl get married. Girl is a Christian, boy is not. Girl grows in one direction with one set of goals and standards while boy grows in the opposite direction with conflicting goals and standards. Boy and girl divorce with much heartbreak. I would imagine that when the apostle Paul advised against being yoked together with unbelievers (2 Cor. 6:14), he was writing out of his own experience of watching the heartache and confusion of "unequally yoked" *(KJV)* or "mismated" *(RSV)* people trying to have good marriages.

Scott Kirby gives what I think to be very sound advice in his book *Dating:* "Human beings are composed of body, soul and spirit. When a Christian marries a non-

Christian, the most they can have is two-thirds of a relationship."[1] I would simply add this: If you date non-Christians you are playing with fire. And not for the reason that they'll take you straight to hell. You are playing with fire because, while you may be very much alike, you are very different at the same time. Also, why settle for second best when you can have God's best in your life?

At this point, you might be objecting because I keep talking about marriage. You might even be saying, "There aren't any Christian guys or girls around here for me to date." I like Kirby's response: "If you usually date non-Christians, then chances are you will marry a non-Christian."[2] As I've said, the Bible is very clear when it comes to believers marrying non-Christians: "Do not be mismated with unbelievers. For what partnership have righteousness and iniquity? Or what fellowship has light with darkness?" (2 Cor. 6:14, *RSV*). Two people having two separate sets of goals and two separate "lords" will have a difficult time ever really coming together and developing a strong marriage.

My goal in this chapter has been to get you to think about what is best for you and your relationship with God. I caution you to think through your dating relationships seriously. It could mean the difference between a happy, fulfilled future and a future of disappointment and misery. When it comes to dating, don't settle for second best!

* THINGS TO THINK ABOUT *

- What advice would you give a person who is ready to date but is not being asked out?
- Which suggestions on dating found in this chapter are most helpful for you? Why?
- Name two or three date ideas from the list in this chapter that appeal to you and that cost little or nothing.
- What is your opinion about dating non-Christians? On what facts and experiences is your opinion based?

* RESPECT BUILDERS *

1. Make your own list of creative, fun and enjoyable dates. You might want to arrange your creative ideas into categories:

Least expensive date
Most outrageous date
First date
Group dates

2. Avoid dating non-Christians. When you put this statement in black and white, it sounds harsh. But remember, you are not being urged to avoid *friendships* with non-Christians. God loves them, and He wants to love them through you. But dating is a very special kind of relationship—and evidence shows that it does lead to marriage!

If you're not sure what the Bible says about marrying non-Christians, read 2 Corinthians 6:14. Based on this verse, what are some reasons for not marrying a person who isn't a Christian?

* TEAM EFFORT *

How Christians are to treat each other:

Review Ephesians 4 and 5. These chapters talk about unity among believers and about how Christians are to live. The passage culminates with a beautiful description of Christian marriage. And remember while you're reading this, that everything Scripture says about how Christians in general are to treat each other applies to Christian marriage partners (and dating as well)!

In the following chart, list instructions from Ephesians 4 and 5 for how Christians are to treat each other. (I've given you a running start.)

HOW CHRISTIANS ARE TO TREAT EACH OTHER
Humbly
Gently

PARTIES

When the phone rang, it was Jill's mother. (Jill was one of the 16-year-old girls in my youth group.) As I talked to her on the phone, Jill's mother seemed a little pushy and a little desperate. She told me that recently Jill had "really changed for the worse." Jill was partying all the time, was losing interest in school and had a bad attitude around the house. Her mother said that I had to help her wayward daughter and asked when I could meet with her.

It usually takes awhile to get going in a counseling session. When a parent makes the appointment, the young person rarely wants to see me if he or she doesn't know me, and often he or she expects me to side with the parents—which I don't always do! But Jill and I hit if off almost immediately. She confided that she had been apprehensive about meeting me and I confided that I'd been apprehensive about meeting her, too!

After all the terrible things her mother had said, I couldn't believe this was her daughter! Jill was open, honest, polite and very friendly. This fact said to me that although she might have a bad attitude at home, she had a lot going for her. I could tell that Jill had as much potential as anyone I had recently met.

We met together a couple of times. Her story was similar to hundreds and hundreds of others. Yes, she was partying a little too much. Yes, she had experimented with drugs and alcohol. Yes, she was having trouble in school, and it was also true that things weren't going well at home. Tension was in the air—but it wasn't all from Jill. Her parents were experiencing a lot of stress at work and in their relationship with each other.

Despite this rather difficult situation, one thing in Jill's favor was that she said she was a Christian. In her words, "I'm not much of a Christian, but I do believe and I have a desire to grow in my faith." I believed her. I believed that she was sincere, and I asked one of our woman advisers to spend some time with her on a one-to-one basis. They went shopping, played a little tennis and even started doing a weekly Bible study together.

It seemed as though things were going much better for Jill. Then late one night,

I got a call from her. She had been to a party, she was very drunk and she needed a ride home. My wife and I got out of bed and went to pick her up. By that time, she had sobered up enough to talk sense, and she definitely needed to talk about things. She had not partied as much lately as she had before. But tonight's party had been important. Most of her friends had planned to attend, and a guy she really liked had kept asking if she was going to be there. He paid a lot of attention to her that night. They drank too much and Jill had blacked out. She was now sobbing in our car: "I think we went all the way, but I don't even remember." Jill was stunned, shocked at herself and very depressed.

One day in my office a few months after what Jill called "the worst night in my life," we were talking about the need to discuss the topic of partying in our youth group. Jill and I came up with these five suggestions, which we titled "Practical Guidelines for Partying." Take the time to read this list. Learn from Jill's experience! Don't wait to learn some of these lessons from personal heartbreak.

Practical Guidelines for Partying

If Partying Is a Weak Point in Your Life, Don't Go to Parties

Even if you enjoy going to parties, but find that you can't seem to control your actions as you would like, don't go. It's not worth the possible pain and hurt you might subject yourself to. Remember that we must live with our choices and their consequences, so choose—an act of your will!—not to go. Also, I think it is important to replace your old negative actions with new positive actions. If, for example, you have been a heavy partier and you want to stop, then don't just spend time watching TV and doing nothing. Replace the time you spent partying with other, more positive activities.

The key word here is "replace." It is much easier to overcome a bad habit or weakness in your life when you replace the negative experience with a positive one. My suggestion is that you write down on a piece of paper alternatives to partying that you would enjoy. Then when the temptation comes and you don't think you can handle the pressure, you can look at other possible options and choose one of those more positive experiences. A good list of possible replacements in the preceding chapter on dating suggests nearly 100 date ideas.

Host "Clean" Parties

It is not necessarily wrong to go to a party. All parties will not bring you down. To party really means to celebrate—and Christians have more to celebrate than anyone I know. Jill suggested that some of the Christians she knew could host what she called "clean" parties. The great thing about a party is spending time with people. Instead of going to parties where you have no control over what will take place, host parties that will be great fun and at the same time will keep you from getting into trouble.

As a Christian, if You Go to Parties, Invite the Lord Jesus to Go with You
Does that sound corny? It shouldn't. If you are a Christian, Jesus wants to be involved in everything in which you are involved. If you actively invite Christ to attend a party with you, this awareness of Him will help you refrain from doing things that might disappoint both you and God. Also, you might be surprised to find that you have a better time than you've ever had!

**Choose Friends Who Will Help You Be the Best Person
You Can Possibly Be**
Jill had to take a serious look at the friends with whom she was spending most of her time. She finally decided that many of her problems stemmed from the kind of people with whom she had been hanging around. At first, she didn't think they were affecting her lifestyle, but when she really thought about it, she realized that she had been compromising many of her beliefs because of peer pressure. Jill decided to choose close friends who would be a better influence on her and whose lifestyle would challenge her to live a more fulfilled life.

Christians Do Not Live by the World's Standards
Jill asked me to add this guideline to the list. Her point is an important one, and perhaps Jesus said it best: "No one can serve two masters. Either he will hate the one and love the other, or he will be devoted to the one and despise the other" (Matt. 6:24). For most of us, "wanting our cake and wanting to eat it, too" describes our desires. Most of us, if we are honest, want to live by the world's standards and also by God's standards. Sometimes we have to decide which is the very best standard to live by, and then go for it. Jill looked at and experienced what the world could offer and what God could offer, and she chose God. She told me not long ago, "Not for one moment have I regretted my choice."

Paul's Words to Us

When God's standards seem rather abstract to us, that is when we need to turn to the Bible. I can think of several paragraphs written by Paul that set forth God's standards for us. These paragraphs really challenged me as a high school student, and they still challenge me today. I encourage you to take the time to read and study Colossians 3:1-17.

Arguing that because "you have been raised with Christ," Paul urges you to "set your hearts on things above, where Christ is seated at the right hand of God. Set your minds on things above, not on earthly things" (vv. 1,2). As he continues, Paul spares no words as he exhorts us, "Put to death, therefore, whatever belongs to your earthly nature" and "put on the new self, which is being renewed in knowledge in the image of its Creator" (vv. 5,10). Paul then offers us some specific instructions:

Therefore, as God's chosen people, holy and dearly loved, clothe your-selves with compassion, kindness, humility, gentleness and patience. Bear with each other and forgive whatever grievances you may have against one another. Forgive as the Lord forgave you. And over all these virtues put on love, which binds them all together in perfect unity (vv. 12-14).

Take time to read and study the Colossians passage in its entirety. Paul clearly defines the high standards we Christians should aim for in our daily lives. These standards should apply to our behavior at parties as much as they should apply to any aspect of our lives. Let me echo Paul as I close the chapter: Choose friends and activities that honor God, don't invite temptation into your life, and trust God to be with you through whatever temptations might still arise.

* THINGS TO THINK ABOUT *

- Do you think Christians should attend parties that offer drugs or drinking? Why or why not?
- What are the pros and cons of attending parties?
- What are some alternative ideas for things to do instead of partying?
- In Colossians 3:1 (quoted in this chapter), Paul tells Christians to "set your hearts on things above." What do you think that means?

* RESPECT BUILDERS *

1. If partying is a weak point in your life, don't go to parties. List at least 10 things you could do instead of going to a party. (See chapter 12 on dating if you need some ideas.)
2. Host "clean" parties. Write a complete plan for a "clean" party you and your friends would enjoy. You might want to decide on a theme. Describe the dec-orations, the refreshments and the activities. Make a list of the people you would like to invite to your party.

Theme
Decorations
Refreshments
Guests
Date and Time

Now clear it with your parents and do it!

* TEAM EFFORT *

Remember that Christians do not live by the world's standards:

Think back to the last party you attended. What sort of standards did people seem to be following? How were these standards and behaviors similar to what God calls us to follow? How were these standards and behaviors different from what God wants our lives to be like?

Summarize your observations and ideas on the following chart and discuss them.

STANDARDS AT THE PARTY	GOD'S STANDARDS

DRUGS AND DRINKING

I'm no prude. In fact, many adults who read this book might think I should be a little more prudish. But I'll be honest with you: Drugs and drinking scare me. Maybe it's because I've seen too many of the negative side effects of drinking in my own family. Maybe it's Steven, whom I met a few years ago. At 16, his brain was fried from putting too many drugs into his body—and he had once had all the potential in the world for leading a happy and fulfilled life. Maybe it's Jill who got drunk and now isn't sure if she is a virgin or not. The list could go on; the stories only get worse, especially when you consider that most of the deaths in automobile accidents are caused by drunk drivers.

I'm also really frightened when it comes to what some people call the "mind benders." I hope you never even experiment with drugs or alcohol. The odds are that by the time you are 18, you will have already tried one, if not both. I'm not going to tell you that every time you drink or take drugs horrible things will happen to you, because they won't.

Consider This...

Think Through Your Actions: Who's in Control?

A person who is high is not in control of his or her actions. Charlie Shedd wrote, "It is a good idea, where sex is involved to keep checking who's in control. Are you doing the thinking or is somebody else doing it for you? Do you really want to do this? Or are you doing it because somebody else is pressuring you?"[1] I've heard far too many stories about people who got high, couldn't control their actions and bingo, a pregnancy occurred—bringing with it all the lifelong effects that come with unwanted pregnancies.

If You Drink, Don't Drive; If You Take Drugs, Don't Drive

I have a name for people who drink and drive: FOOLS.

Science has proven that even one beer can keep some people from being in control of their driving. A drunk driver (and I'm not necessarily talking about the kind of drunk we see in the movies) is not only a dangerous weapon who may kill or maim himself or herself; a drunk driver has the definite ability to kill or maim innocent bystanders. If you drink or take drugs, don't drive.

Many people loved the movie *Arthur*. It was the story of a happy drunk. To be honest, it depressed me greatly. Most drunks aren't *that* happy or *that* cute. Furthermore, most drunk drivers aren't as lucky as Arthur was when he drove through downtown New York City, barely missing other cars and pedestrians. *Arthur* was a make-believe story. If you want the real story, read your newspaper. Drunk-driving accidents happen every day, and most of the time they don't have happy endings.

Alcoholism Is on the Rise

Fifteen percent of today's teenagers are alcoholics. More than 3 million teenagers in the United States today are problem drinkers! They don't look or act like the stereotypical alcoholic. (Few people do!) They are addicted for life to something that has broken up more homes and ruined more lives than anything in the world. If you have even the slightest suspicion that you could possibly be an alcoholic, get help now. Don't wait until you hurt your family or ruin your life. Also, if you want to have an eye-opening experience, visit a local chapter of Alcoholics Anonymous (AA). You'll see very quickly that alcoholics are not happy people until they become recovered alcoholics; even then, many carry the scars of alcoholism for life.

The Bible says, "Don't drink too much wine, for many evils lie along that path; be filled instead with the Holy Spirit, and controlled by him" (Eph. 5:18, *TLB*). I wish the Bible said, "Don't drink or take drugs; they will ruin your life!" But it doesn't. It simply says that we shouldn't get drunk (or high), but that we should be filled instead with the Holy Spirit. When you are high, you definitely cannot be allowing the Holy Spirit of God to work in your life.

I know a young person who chose not to drink when most of his friends and family drank. Some of his very close loved ones were alcoholics. I asked him once, "Why don't you drink?" I will never forget his answer: "I love the taste of some types of alcohol, and there is nothing better on a hot day than a cold glass of beer. *But I've decided I don't need it.* I'm not laying my trip on others, because I'm not convinced that everyone shouldn't drink; but let me tell you why I don't drink or take drugs. I could drink just one beer a week and see nothing wrong with it except that my alcoholic father would see that one beer and use it to justify his *case* of beer. I don't want to have a silent negative witness to my friends or family. And besides all that, I don't need to drink or take drugs to be accepted. I'd rather be in control of my mind, spirit and body at all times."

All I can add to this statement is, "Well said, my friend; I can't think of anyone who wouldn't respect your position."

Drugs

I get nervous about any mood-altering substance. Too many times, I've seen my friends innocently get involved with pot and as a result have their brains "fried" on PCP or acid (LSD). This doesn't mean that everyone who has ever experimented with marijuana will end up in the back of some alley having needle marks up and down his or her arms. Anyone who becomes involved with any mood-altering substance, however, must carefully and logically think through his or her actions.

Here's the straight scoop. Drugs work! They make you feel good and they *will* get you high every single time. Here's the problem. Because drugs alter your mood, a person can easily become dependent on drugs. The fact is that young people who take drugs at an early age often quit coping with stress in a normal way and become dependent on drugs to "make them feel better." After a while, people become preoccupied with getting high because it is the only way they can function. And most of the people who are preoccupied with getting high are not the skid-row bums. They are the people who have normal jobs and semi-normal families. Yet, if you watch them over the years, they bring a great deal of tragedy into their own lives. What does all this mean? I believe there is a reason why they call this stuff "dope"...

I must discuss one more important issue. It is almost universally agreed that there is a biological predisposition to alcoholism and probably drug use.[2] I was speaking recently at a high school, and I said to the students: "There is great evidence today that there is a biological predisposition to the disease of alcoholism. This means alcoholism can be inherited from your family. So if your dad, mom, brothers, sisters, aunts, uncles or grandparents are alcoholics, you have a much greater risk of becoming an alcoholic. Your body will crave alcohol differently from other people's."

After the assembly, a young man walked up to me and said, "What you are telling me is that if my dad is an alcoholic, then I'm at greater risk to become an alcoholic and I should not drink."

I nodded my head. "Yes, that's pretty much what I'm trying to get across."

He said, "That's not fair!"

I replied, "Who said anything about life being fair?"

As we continued to talk, I assessed that my friend was already a budding alcoholic. He told me he could drink five cans of beer or four to six wine coolers and not get drunk. Then he added, "But you probably don't believe that."

I smiled and said, "No, I absolutely believe you, and that proves my point that you are most probably already an alcoholic." He looked at me, confused. I went on, "Alcoholics have a very *high tolerance* for alcohol consumption. You can drink differently from your friends because your body is addicted to alcohol. People with a high tolerance for alcohol, people who can 'hold their liquor,' simply drink under their tolerance level. But eventually their bodies will break down and their tolerance levels will change, or they will drink over their tolerance level and major problems will occur."

My friend shook my hand, gave me an understanding look, and walked away. I hope he quits drinking or he will find himself being one more negative statistic.

My cry to students today is, *Reconsider your drinking or drugging habits.* I choose not to have even one drink and, of course, no drugs. I can only say that anyone who takes on a lifestyle of abstinence from drugs or alcohol will never, never regret it. That's more than I can say for the drinkers and drug users who suffer from out-of-control decisions. Think about it.

✳ THINGS TO THINK ABOUT ✳

- Why do you think some young people drink enough to get drunk?
- Are most teenagers able to control their drinking and drugs? Why or why not?
- Which philosophy of drinking do you feel closest to at this time of your life:

    (_____) Never touch the stuff!
    (_____) People can drink but not in excess.
    (_____) It's a free country: people have the right to drink as much as they want.

- Without mentioning names, do you know of anyone who has had a negative experience with drugs or drinking? How has this affected your own thoughts about using drugs or alcohol?
- Do you think smoking marijuana is more harmful or less harmful than drinking alcohol? Why?

✳ RESPECT BUILDERS ✳

1. Think through your actions and realize who is in control.

    - Can you be completely in control when you drink or take drugs?
    - What are some disadvantages or dangers of being out of control?
    - Read Ephesians 5:18. What does this verse mean?

2. If you drink, don't drive; if you take drugs, don't drive. List some guidelines you might need to follow if you drink or take drugs and then realize you should not drive.

    The guidelines you just wrote down also apply if you are a passenger and the driver of the car starts drinking or taking drugs. *Do not ride with this person.* Make sure you have an alternative plan. Write down that alternative plan.

3. What are some of the reasons the word "dope" is an appropriate name for drugs?

* TEAM EFFORT *

The "Just Say No" game is an excellent way to help you practice saying no to drugs.

The "Just Say No" Game[3]

The object of the game is to respond to a high-pressure situation in such a way that those applying pressure will back off. Try to develop several creative ways to say no.

Drug Offers

1. You are at school in between classes, and someone asks you to walk into the bathroom to smoke a joint.
2. A boy you know says he snuck two of his mother's tranquilizers out of the medicine cabinet and asks you to meet him after school to ingest them.
3. One of the high school seniors offers to give you a ride home and tells you he has some pure and expensive crack.
4. At one of the local hangouts, a girl offers you a red pill and promises it will make you feel as though you are in another world.
5. You see a friend under the football stadium, shooting something in his arm. He offers to let you try it free.

Alcohol Offers

1. Your older brother and his friend pick you up from a party, and his friend offers you a cold beer for the trip home.
2. At a party, the gang gets into the parents' liquor cabinet. Everyone starts drinking out of the bottle of vodka.
3. Your parents take you out to a nice dinner at a local club. Your dad orders something to drink for everyone and tells you it is okay for you to have one.
4. On the drive home from school, one of the people you consider to be your friend pulls out a bottle of champagne and pops the cork, asking you to drink up.
5. On a fishing trip, you go up the river with your brother. You are in the middle of the forest, and he says that because no one is around you can have a beer.

GUILT AND FORGIVENESS

Buffy is a seven-month-old puppy whose favorite meals are flowers, curtains and tennis shoes. Every day, my wife, Cathy, and I yell at Buffy and threaten her within an inch of her life. But it doesn't seem to help much. She just keeps chewing on anything and everything.

Here's a funny thing about Buffy, though. She almost seems to *know* when she has done something wrong. As soon as she has torn up my newest jogging shoes or eaten all the daisies Cathy put on the coffee table, she runs and hides under the kitchen table. And there she sits looking as innocent as she can and trying to pretend nothing has happened.

But Cathy and I are wise to Buffy. We know that if that dog is under the kitchen table, it means that she has been up to no good. Sure enough, we don't have to look very hard to find evidence of Buffy's most recent mischief. We human beings are a lot like Buffy. We do wrong things, and then we feel guilty for what we've done. We have guilty consciences.

Dr. James Dobson tells about a poll in which kids were asked, "What is conscience?" One six-year-old girl said a conscience is the spot inside that "burns if you're not good." A six-year-old boy said he didn't know, but thought it had something to do with feeling bad when you "kicked girls or little dogs." And a nine-year-old explained it as a voice inside that says "no" when you want to do something like beat up your little brothers.[1] One junior higher I know answered the same question by saying that a guilty conscience was "that sick feeling in the pit of your stomach when you realize you've just blown it."

Guilt, however, can be positive. Can you imagine what this world would be like if people didn't have consciences and didn't feel guilty when they did wrong? If human beings felt no guilt, the world probably wouldn't make it through another day. It would explode with sin.[2]

Thousands and thousands of people are committed to mental hospitals today because for one reason or another, they aren't able to deal with their feelings of guilt. I wish these people could understand that although guilt feelings have a necessary role in our lives, the great news of the gospel of Jesus Christ is that we can be *forgiven*. The guilt that drives us to seek forgiveness is then washed away.

I believe many people do not become Christians because they can't believe that the good news—the gospel—of Jesus Christ is true. They keep waiting for the catch to the story. But there is no catch. In Jesus Christ we can find forgiveness for our sins—past, present and future! His death on the cross was the penalty He paid for your sins; the resurrection from the tomb was His victory over sin and death and the gift of life for you. I know that idea is hard to understand, but, nevertheless, it is the truth. Consider the following story.

Sharon's Story

Sharon grew up in a basic middle-class American home. Her family seemed to fight more than the average family, but it was pretty much a normal family. They were not necessarily Christians, but in seventh grade Sharon went to church camp and decided to give her life to Jesus Christ. She became active in her church youth group, but peer pressure began to get to her and she experimented with light drugs and sex. One night when she was a tenth grader, she got a little high and her twelfth-grade boyfriend convinced her to "go all the way." It was against her Christian principles, but she did it anyway. From that time on, she seemed to slip downhill emotionally. Life went on, but this one negative experience paralyzed her faith, her belief in herself and her emotions.

I talked with her when she was in her early 20s. She still seemed paralyzed by guilt. After listening to her story for a long time, I asked her if she had ever asked Jesus Christ to forgive her for this past sin that kept haunting her. She replied, "Yes, almost every day since it happened in tenth grade." Eight years later, she was still pleading for God's forgiveness.

I then asked her what I thought was a simple question: "Do you believe God has forgiven you?"

Her answer gave me insight into her problem. She replied, "I really don't see how He could ever forgive me."

Although Sharon was a Christian, she didn't understand the core of the gospel of Jesus Christ. We all do some pretty rotten things in life, but there is absolutely nothing that God will not forgive. God forgave our sins now and forever because of the sacrifice of Jesus on the cross.

Sharon needed to know—*really* know and believe in her innermost heart—that the very first time she asked for God's forgiveness, He had completely forgiven her. Her problem was that she would not accept His forgiveness and she wouldn't forgive herself. Therefore, she carried around a load of *false* guilt that was ruining her life.

As you can see, God's ways are different from our ways. Humans tend to hold grudges and break off relationships. God, however, always forgives. He always works to give His children new lives. If you have not yet asked Jesus Christ to become part of your life, these next two paragraphs are for you.

Invite Christ into Your Life

The ultimate act of love was Jesus' death on the cross for you. The Bible says, "God demonstrates his own love for us in this: While we were still sinners, Christ died for us" (Rom. 5:8). I believe the most important decision in life is to acknowledge Christ's work on the cross and to invite Him to live within you. When you invite Christ to live in your life, He does a number of things immediately. I'll mention just a few: He forgives your sins; He dwells within you; He gives you eternal life; and He offers you an abundant life on earth.

If you have never asked Jesus Christ to come into your life, I urge you to do so right now. If you say the following simple prayer to God sincerely, your life will literally be transformed from the inside out. If you do say this prayer to God, then I urge you to get involved with Christians who will help you understand your new faith and will help you to grow as a new, forgiven believer. Here's the prayer:

> Almighty God, I love You. Thank You for the supreme sacrifice of love in Jesus Christ's death on the cross. I ask Jesus to come into my life and to forgive my sins. Thank You for setting me free. Amen.

Eventually, Sharon did work through her guilt feelings and accepted the freedom and forgiveness Jesus offers. Today she is a happy, vibrant woman who understands that the forgiveness of Jesus Christ is a *free* gift given to all who ask. The Bible says, "If we confess our sins, he is faithful and just and will forgive us our sins and purify us from all unrighteousness" (1 John 1:9).

Perhaps you are a believer who has a story similar to Sharon's. Now is the time to get rid of your guilt by asking Jesus Christ to forgive your sins. He is faithful to forgive you 100 percent of the time. When you ask, He forgives you, and you never have to feel guilty again.

One time someone asked me, "Aren't you afraid that kids will sin more if you tell them about God's complete forgiveness?"

I replied, "Of course not! When a person really understands the unconditional love and forgiveness of Jesus Christ, the desire for obedience will be greater than the desire to sin." And I pray that you will believe this good news of Jesus Christ so that you will no longer be paralyzed by your guilt. The gift of forgiveness is yours for the asking. How can you pass up such an offer of love and total acceptance?

* THINGS TO THINK ABOUT *

- Why is it so difficult to overcome our guilt feelings?
- Think of Sharon's inability to completely believe that God forgave her. What are some specific differences between real guilt and false guilt?
- What makes it difficult for you to accept God's forgiveness?
- What would you tell someone who has a guilty conscience?

* RESPECT BUILDERS *

1. All human beings have experienced and many continue to experience guilt for a variety of sins in their lives. In His great love, God provides a way for us to leave behind our guilt. He promises us forgiveness for our sins. There is no limit to this forgiveness. We need only to confess our failings to Him, and He gladly forgives us.

   Take a moment to write on a piece of paper every sin that comes to your mind. Ask God to forgive you of your sin and cleanse your life. Remember, His forgiveness is for the asking. Then either tear up, burn or throw away the paper as a sign of God's complete forgiveness.

2. Here are some questions that will help you deal with forgiving others:

   - When have you struggled to forgive someone? Be specific about the circumstances.
   - Why was it hard for you to forgive that person? What were you feeling?
   - When have you asked for forgiveness for something you said or did? Describe the situation.
   - How did you feel about approaching the person you had hurt or disappointed?
   - What is the greatest act of forgiveness by any ordinary human being that you know about personally?

* TEAM EFFORT *

A Bible study on forgiveness:

The story of David and Bathsheba in 2 Samuel 11—12 illustrates how even great men of God make mistakes. Read the story as a group, and then let each person share what he or she thinks caused David to do the things he did.

To conclude this discussion, read through Psalm 51. Ask the group how the emotions of guilt and pain David experienced relate to their lives.

What do these verses say about God?

Psalm 86:5

Psalm 103:3

What did God do that we might be forgiven and live in a right relationship with Him?

John 3:16

Romans 5:8

What does God do with our confessed sin?

1 John 1:9

Once a sin is confessed and forgiven, does God remember it? Look up the following verses. Write them down to impress upon your mind what God does with confessed, forgiven sin.

Psalm 103:12

Isaiah 43:25

Micah 7:19

If God forgets your sins and buries them in the sea, there is never any reason for you to go fishing for them!

OPTIONS FOR THE PREGNANT

One of the reasons I've written this book is so that the subject of this chapter will never become a reality in your life. Unfortunately, in the United States alone more than 1 million unwed girls and women become pregnant each year—and the number is increasing rapidly. Far too many times (perhaps most of the time), the people involved have not thought through the options until it is too late. Furthermore, often the pregnant girl must make some difficult decisions on her own because her partner has conveniently removed himself from the scene and is nowhere to be found.

To be honest, all the options for an unwed mother-to-be are lousy. All the options are complicated. All the options will cause a great deal of hurt and pain. Sometimes the difficulties are so great that the girls simply won't admit they are pregnant. They repress every thought about the subject until they actually believe they are not pregnant—even after "the signs" begin to show. Too many girls do not make decisions about their pregnancies because they simply wish it to go away. But it won't.

What can you do if you are pregnant? Here are some steps to take.

Helpful Steps for Pregnant Girls

First of all, take a pregnancy test. Be 100 percent sure you are pregnant. If you have had sexual intercourse and have missed your period or if you are even a little late, get checked as soon as possible. There is no sense in second-guessing your body. The sooner you know for sure, the more time you will have to think through your options.

Today there are many easy ways to find out if you are pregnant. It takes approximately 10 days after intercourse to know for sure, and methods are being researched as of this writing that could possibly reveal a pregnancy as early as 5 days after conception. Early Pregnancy Tests (EPTs) are available without a prescription at local drugstores, or you can go to your doctor, a hospital out-patient clinic or a free clinic in your local area. If you use the Early Pregnancy Test and it indicates you are pregnant, then you should immediately go to your doctor for confirmation and for instruction in prenatal care.

If you find out you are pregnant, don't suffer alone. Share your situation with a person you trust. The best option is to sit down with one or both of your parents and have a heart-to-heart, open and honest conversation. Nine times out of 10, you'll find that you will receive more support than you expected. If you can't talk with your parents, find someone—a youth worker at church, a counselor at school or a trusted adult friend—in whom to confide. You need all the positive support you can get.

Then take a serious look at the options as rationally as possible. During stressful times, people often make emotional decisions that are simply wrong choices. They mean well, but fail to carefully consider all the options because of the emotional tension in their lives.

Linda's Lament

At the age of 25, Linda told me her own story of sadness and grief. When she was 18, she was homecoming queen, cheerleader and president of her church's youth group. She became pregnant by an older man who immediately told her she must get an abortion. Linda was confused, scared and empty. Without telling family or friends, she went to another county in her state and had an abortion. It has been seven years and Linda has still not told her friends or family. Of course, her "boyfriend" is long gone. She told me she really regretted having an abortion. She called it a "form of murder." Linda cried, "I may never be able to forgive myself." She never dreamed she would be unmarried and pregnant. When she found herself in that predicament, she felt forced into aborting her baby. Now she lives to regret her actions.

I've heard too many similar stories. It always seems as though it is the good, well-meaning people who make mistakes by never dealing with all the options.

Choosing an Option Intelligently

My wife and I sat with Janet and Bart. They were both 19 years old, intelligent, athletic, attractive, not married and very (eight and a half months) pregnant. They were dealing with the difficult process of deciding whether to keep their baby or give the baby up for adoption. Neither choice was easy, and either one would change their lives forever. Their social worker and my wife and I, however, sensed that although they were confused, eventually Janet and Bart would make the decision that would be right for them. They were thinking rationally and looking at the options despite the intense emotional nature of the situation.

Ultimately, Janet and Bart did give up the baby for adoption to two very special Christian parents who are making a wonderful home for this baby. I appreciated the maturity Janet and Bart displayed as they took the time to work through the options confronting them.

Let's take a closer look at the options. The three possible options are abortion, adoption and keeping the child. All three options have unique problems but all three are options you must consider. This chapter will deal with two of the options, and the next chapter will deal with abortion.

Options to Consider

Adoption

Although adoption is not as popular as it used to be, it is definitely still an important option. Adoption can be a positive alternative to abortion or keeping the baby. It can be a positive experience for the birth parents, the child and the adoptive parents.

At 17, Anne thought she was too young to raise the child she was carrying. Her boyfriend was being supportive to her through the pregnancy, but he wasn't ready to settle down. Seeking the help of a counselor, Anne carefully considered the options and decided to give up her baby for adoption. The adoptive parents were a young couple in their late 20s. They had been married for five years and had been told they would never be able to have children of their own. They desperately wanted to raise children and give them a home. A medical doctor made the arrangements for Anne's baby to be adopted by this couple. Anne was reassured that her child would be given to very special people who would provide a warm, loving home for the baby. When she delivered, Anne allowed the adoptive parents to take the baby home from the hospital. Later, Anne wrote a letter to the new parents and mailed it to her doctor who sent it on to the couple. This is what she wrote:

> Dear Parents of the Little Baby:
> I want you to know that I pray for your—I mean "our"—child daily. As I look back on the decision to give up my baby for adoption, it was the most difficult decision I've ever made.
> But I want you to know, too, that it was also the wisest decision and I know the best decision for the baby. I hope you'll tell the baby when he grows up that I love him and will always love him. Help him understand that I gave him up because I wanted the best for him.
> Even though I've never met you and probably never will, I'm grateful to God for the love you have for "our" child.
>
> With all my love,
> Unsigned

Should you decide to give up your baby for adoption, make sure you select a respectable agency whose number one desire is to give your baby the finest home possible. Make sure the agency, lawyer or whoever handles the adoption does a thorough home study of the adoptive family. One of the biggest issues in the mind of every birth parent is whether the baby will live in a happy, secure home that is filled with love and support. When a person is confident that the baby will be in such a home, it is easier to give up the baby to adoptive parents.

Keeping the Baby
An option that seems to be gaining in popularity among young people is keeping the baby. Today more than ever before, we see young girls deciding against abortion or adoption; instead, they are raising their babies themselves. Here I have mixed emotions. If a young person can handle the responsibility of child raising, she should strongly consider keeping the baby. Most young people, however, have a terribly difficult time managing their own problems let alone constant pleas for love and attention. I'm amazed at the amount of child abuse that consequently occurs among teenage parents. The statistics are frightening.

If you are pregnant and are trying to make a decision about keeping the baby, ask yourself questions such as these: What is the best for the baby? Will I get married to the father? Am I emotionally stable enough to handle the constant demands of child raising? Also, make sure you get help from a counselor. I know several great kids who were born to teenage parents and who have turned out fine. I also know some young people who have been raised by teenage parents and who have had real emotional struggles because of being raised in a difficult home situation. Your decision to keep the child must be a personal decision, but get the advice and help of people who sincerely love you and want the best for you and the baby.

Charlie Shedd wrote a great book on sex entitled *The Stork is Dead*. Written in 1968, it still offers what seems to be timeless insight. He quotes, for instance, a letter written to him by a young girl on what it's like to be married at age 17. It's worth reprinting here.

Jimmy and I couldn't wait so now we are married. Big deal!

Let me tell you what it is like to be married at 17. It is like living in this dump on the third floor up and your only window looks out on somebody else's third floor dump.

It is like coming home at night so tired you feel like you're dead from standing all day at your checker's job. But you don't dare sit down because you might never get up again and there are so many things to do like cooking and washing and dusting and ironing. So you go through the motions and you hate your job and you ask yourself, "Why don't I quit?" and you already know why. It's because there are grocery bills and drug bills and rent bills and doctor bills, and Jimmy's crummy little check from the lumber yard won't cover them, that's why!

Then you try to play with the baby until Jimmy comes home. Only sometimes you don't feel like playing with her. But even if you do, you get this awful feeling that you are only doing it because you feel guilty. She is so beautiful, and you know it isn't fair for her to be in that old lady's nursery all day long. Then you wash diapers and mix formula and you hate it, and you wonder how long it will be till she can tell how you feel, and wouldn't it be awful if she could tell already?

Then Jimmy doesn't come home, and you know it's because he is out with the boys doing the things he didn't get to do because you had to get married. So, finally you go to bed and cry yourself to sleep telling yourself that it really is better when he doesn't come because sometimes he says the cruelest things. Then you ask yourself "Why does he hate me so?" And you know it is because he feels trapped, and he doesn't love you anymore, like he said he would.

Then he comes home and he wakes you up, and he starts saying all the nice things he said before you got married. But you know it is only because he wants something, and yet you want to believe that maybe it is the old Jimmy again. So you give in, only when he gets what he wants, he turns away and you know he was only using you once more. So you try to sleep but you can't. This time, you cry silently because you don't want to admit that you care.

You lie there and think. You think about your parents and your brothers and the way they teased you. You think about your backyard and the swing and the tree house and all the things you had when you were little. You think about the good meals your mother cooked and how she tried to talk to you, but you were so sure she had forgotten what it was like to be in love.

Then you think about your girlfriends and the fun they must be having at the prom. You think about the college you planned to go to, and you wonder who will get the scholarship they promised you. You wonder who you would have dated in college and who you might have married and what kind of a job would he have had?

Suddenly you want to talk, so you reach over and touch Jimmy. But he is far away and he pushes you aside, so now you can cry yourself to sleep for real.

If you ever meet any girls like me who think they are just too smart to listen to anyone, I hope you'll tell them that this is what it is like to be married at seventeen.[1]

As this story, and the entire chapter, has pointed out, the decision facing unwed teenage mothers is not an easy one. If you find yourself in this situation, it is important that you think through the options as carefully and as unemotionally as possible. It is also important that you really try to listen to the advice of those people who care about you and whom you can trust. Also, lean on God for His strength in this difficult time, for His answers to your prayers for guidance and for the peace He offers to His children.

* THINGS TO THINK ABOUT *

- Why do you think some girls deny they are pregnant?
- Who do you know who would be helpful to talk to about subjects such as this? Consider, for example, your parents, youth worker, minister, a school counselor or an adult friend.
- What advice would you give a girl who is pregnant?
- Read Psalm 139:13-17. How do these verses relate to a couple who is making a decision about a pregnancy?

* RESPECT BUILDERS *

1. Read Psalm 139. Jot down some sentences and phrases that speak of God's love and concern for you.
2. Visit a Christian crisis pregnancy center with a friend, your youth group or a family member and ask for a presentation on options for people who are pregnant. You may even want to invite them to make a presentation at your church or school.

* TEAM EFFORT *

To consider the pros and cons of adoption and keeping the baby, complete the following chart. List arguments for and against each choice from the viewpoint of the baby's mother, the baby's father, the baby's grandparents (that is, the parents of the baby's father and mother), and the baby himself/herself. Discuss these with your group.

	ADOPTION	KEEPING THE BABY
Baby's Mother Pros		
Cons		

	ADOPTION	KEEPING THE BABY
Baby's Father Pros		
Cons		
Baby's Grandparents Pros		
Cons		
Baby Pros		
Cons		

WHAT ABOUT ABORTION?

Seldom in our nation's history has there been a more emotional issue than that of abortion. I realize you may be receiving some confusing and contradictory information. In our fallen world, whether we like it or not, abortion has become an option. *However,* let me say it as clearly as I can: In my opinion abortion is *not* an option. My heart bleeds for young women who get pregnant out of wedlock, and I feel deeply for women who have already chosen to abort their babies. I know it's a complicated decision. Yet, the fact remains that regardless of the circumstances of pregnancy, the baby developing inside the womb is a person who deserves as much attention and protection as his or her mother.

Some people will tell you the baby is only a fetus and not a person. Yet, on day one of the pregnancy the "sperm joins with the ovum (egg) to form one cell. This new life has inherited 23 chromosomes from each parent, 46 in all. This one cell contains the complex genetic blueprint for every detail of human development—the child's sex, hair and eye color, height and skin tone."[1]

That's all on the first day! At 3 weeks old, the heart is already beating. Brain waves can be detected and recorded at 40 days old. At just more than 12 weeks, the baby sleeps, awakens and can actually exercise its muscles. Fine hair has already begun to grow on the baby's head.

Cathy and I began to feel our daughter's movements by four-and-a-half months. Many people still get abortions at four-and-a-half months! I personally know women who have had abortions. They have confided to me that they can't forget the abortion no matter how hard they try. The term for this is "postabortion syndrome." Often a woman who has had an abortion will suffer deep grief about the loss of her baby. She will struggle with intense fear, anger, sadness and guilt, knowing she has allowed a living baby in her womb to be killed.

Choosing Life

Pamela was one of the leaders in our youth group. She wanted to become either a youth worker in the church or an attorney. Pamela got great grades. She was loved by her peers and was one of my favorite people. When she came into my office and told me she was pregnant, I was shocked. She had experimented with sexual intercourse one time, got pregnant, and now had come to tell me she was going to get an abortion.

Pamela said, "I know how you feel about abortion, Jim, but I wanted to tell someone before I did it. My parents (who were leaders in our church) would be embarrassed. I want to go on to college and if I had a baby my life would be ruined forever." What would you have said to Pamela if you were me?

First, I assured her I loved her. I thanked her for sharing her problem with me. She did most of the talking, and it was important for me to listen. After all, listening is the language of love. Finally, when she had said what was on her mind, she asked for my opinion.

That afternoon in my office we discussed all the issues. How would she feel about herself because in her heart she knew she had a baby inside her? This wasn't just tissue, and she knew it deep down. We talked about sharing the issue of her pregnancy with her parents. Sure they would be disappointed, but not half as disappointed as if they knew she was getting an abortion. We discussed the other options of keeping the baby or giving the baby a wonderful home through adoption. I shared with her Cathy's and my struggle with infertility and the strong desire to adopt a child. We talked on and on.

Pamela admitted that in the strong emotional turmoil of her life she had not taken some of these factors into consideration. It was important for Pamela to look at all sides of the issue. Because Pamela was a Christian, it was important to look at the Bible. Together Pamela and I read:

So God created man in his own image, in the image of God he created him; male and female he created them (Gen. 1:27).

Sons are a heritage from the Lord, children a reward from him (Ps. 127:3).

For you created my inmost being; you knit me together in my mother's womb. I praise you because I am fearfully and wonderfully made; your works are wonderful, I know that full well. My frame was not hidden from you when I was made in the secret place. When I was woven together in the depths of the earth, your eyes saw my unformed body. All the days ordained for me were written in your book before one of them came to be (Ps. 139:13-16).

Listen to me, you islands, hear this, you distant nations: Before I was born the Lord called me; from my birth he has made mention of my name (Isa. 49:1).

For by him all things were created: things in heaven and on earth, visible and invisible, whether thrones or powers or rulers or authorities; all things were created by him and for him (Col. 1:16).

After looking at the Scripture references, Pamela and I prayed and cried. I asked her if she was willing to give this baby in her "tummy" over to God. She nodded. That evening, together, we talked with her parents. They were shocked, yes, but more understanding than Pamela imagined.

Pamela made an appointment with an excellent Christian crisis pregnancy center. After much counsel, many difficult decisions and an incredible amount of support, Pamela chose to give up her baby for adoption. Today, years later, Pamela is helping other unwed mothers. She is happily married and a deeply committed Christian. Today, somewhere in a Christian home a little boy has two parents who love him and are raising their "Matthew," which means gift from God. Thank God for Pamela. Thank God she had the courage to make the right decision and not necessarily the easy decision.

One last thought. I have this feeling if Jesus Christ were here He would say, "I died to redeem the lost; the crippled; the sinners; and the innocent, defenseless babies who are in the wombs of mothers." I think He would stand loud and clear on the side of protecting innocent, unborn babies because they, too, have the incredible potential of someday becoming instruments of the kingdom of God.

Please don't sit on the fence on this issue. Make a decision that abortion is not an option for you. Choose life.

* THINGS TO THINK ABOUT *

- What makes abortion the easy way out of the problem but not the right way?
- What do you suppose God's view of abortion is?
- Why do you think abortion is such a controversial subject?
- Why was Pamela's decision to give her baby to God and not get an abortion a difficult one? What were the positive consequences of her decision?

* RESPECT BUILDERS *

1. Make a decision to choose life and stand on the side of innocent, unborn children. You can do this by (a) never being involved in an abortion yourself; (b) working to make sure people hear the side of the unborn; and (c) praying and caring for the burdens of unwed mothers and fathers.
2. Acquire some excellent resources on abortion and become acquainted with the important issues around this significant subject. Here's a partial list of resources:

Booklets

Abortion: A Moral Outrage by Dr. James Dobson (Focus on the Family).
One Church's Answer to Abortion by Bill Hybels (Moody Press).

Books

Abortion: A Relational Look at an Emotional Issue by R. C. Sproul (NavPress, 1990).
Abortion: The Silent Holocaust by John Powell (Tabor Publishing, 1981).
Just Like Ice Cream by Lissa Halls Johnson (Bantam Books, 1984).

Films and Videos

A Question of Worth by Dr. James Dobson (Focus on the Family).
The Eclipse of Reason by Dr. Bernard Nathanson (Bernadell, Inc.).
The Silent Scream by Dr. Bernard Nathanson (American Portrait Films).
Your Crisis Pregnancy by Jane Chastain and Dr. James Dobson (American Portrait Films).

* TEAM EFFORT *

Case Study: Values

Suzanne was 17 and had a lot going in her favor. She was an intelligent and beautiful girl. School work had always been easy for her. Her nearly straight-A average indicated that she was a perfect candidate for an Ivy League university. She dreamed of becoming a lawyer and a politician.

Suzanne was respected by her peers and was sought after as a friend. She had dated several guys from her youth group and church during the past year and a half. Suzanne began dating a young man she met at church who was in the military service. His name was Bob. He was a nice person who had recently moved to her community from another state. He was lonely and loved the positive atmosphere of Suzanne's circle of friends, church and home.

A few months after her relationship with Bob became serious, Suzanne came to the office of her youth worker. It was easy to tell she had been crying for hours. Between sobs, she blurted out this story: "Bob and I went 'all the way' once. That month I missed my period but I didn't think much about it. The next month I missed my period and went to a doctor. I am pregnant. I told Bob. He gave me $100 for an abortion and told me he is transferring away from the area and never wants to see me again. I don't want to tell my family. And I don't want to carry a baby and be a disgrace to all I've stood for. If I keep the baby, I'll ruin my chances for going to law school."

Although Suzanne had never been a supporter of abortion, she shared with her youth worker that she had made an appointment to get one in two days.

1. What factors in Suzanne's situation added to her feeling of hurt?
2. Because Suzanne had already made an appointment for an abortion, what might she have been seeking from her youth worker?
3. If you were the youth worker, what would you say? What would you do?
4. In what ways might Suzanne's parents react? How might their reactions affect Suzanne?
5. Read Psalm 139:13-16. How does this passage relate to this case study?

MASTURBATION

The sound of the word "masturbation" causes strange reactions in most people. Masturbation is, however, an experience most people have had, yet seldom does anyone talk about it. And when so-called experts discuss or write about the subject, they can't seem to agree on whether it is right or wrong.

Some people are uncertain about what masturbation actually is. Technically, masturbation is called "auto-eroticism." "Auto" means "self" and "eroticism" means "sexual stimulation." Put the words together and you have "self sexual stimulation." Masturbation is usually the first sexual behavior for both males and females. Often you'll find little children handling their genitals and exploring their bodies, but even then their parents may discourage this behavior.

About 15 years ago, I was a counselor at a Christian camp. I was working with eight high school guys. Somehow, in our morning Bible study time, the subject of masturbation came up. Before lunch, the word was out: "Jim is willing to talk about masturbation!" Before lunch was finished, the man in charge of the camp had pulled me aside to ask just what we were talking about during the Bible study hour. I told him the same thing I told the guys in my cabin and I am telling you. Incidentally, before the camp had ended, at least 20 high schoolers asked if they could talk with me privately about their problem. This experience says to me that it is time we become more open about this important subject and help people deal with their "problem" in an intelligent manner.

Almost all people have had a masturbation experience by the time they reach 18 years of age. A person is not abnormal if he or she has never had the experience and a person is not abnormal if he or she has had it. Statistics tell us that in the last 25 years, many more girls have masturbated than ever before. I've read statistics that say between 50 and 80 percent of all girls have had a masturbation experience. I've heard it said that 92 percent of all males have had the experience and the other 8 percent are liars. In other words, almost all males have had the experience. I tell you these statistics because far too many people believe they are among just a few people in the world masturbating. They are completely wrong.

"Okay, Jim, but let's get to the point: is masturbation wrong? Is it a sin?" If I must be pinned down, I believe that not all masturbation is necessarily sinful. However, you must make up your own mind. You must intelligently work through the decision. And I would suggest that you turn to God for help. Let me give you two opposing viewpoints from two outstanding Christian people to help you arrive at your decision.

Opposing Views on Masturbation

First, in his book *This Is Loving?*, David Wilkerson says, "Masturbation is not a gift of God for sex drives. Masturbation is not moral behavior and is not condoned in the Scriptures....Masturbation is not harmless fun."[1] On the other hand, Dr. Charlie Shedd, a very respected Christian authority on sex and dating, does call masturbation a "gift of God." He claims that masturbation "can be a positive factor in your total development" and goes on to say that "teenage masturbation is preferable to teenage intercourse. It is better to come home hot and bothered than satisfied and worried."[2]

My own view is somewhere in between these two extremes. Masturbation is practically universal. It isn't the gross sin some think it is, yet at times it can have a negative side to it.

Negative Factors of Masturbation

Specifically, uncontrolled masturbation can be very negative. Psychologists call this kind of behavior "obsessive-compulsive." This means that a person can become so consumed with masturbation that it literally takes over his or her mind and actions. One young man confided to me that he figured he masturbated 10 to 15 times a week and that this one experience had literally taken over his mind. He had tremendous guilt feelings, was drawing more and more into himself, and was afraid to be with people. His obsessive-compulsive behavior was destroying his self-image, his relationship with God and his relationships with other people. We had to help him work through his negative habit and change his behavior.

Another negative effect is uncontrolled fantasy. Jesus loves us unconditionally and yet He calls us to high standards. When discussing the question of lust, for instance, Jesus said, "You have heard that it was said, 'Do not commit adultery.' But I tell you that anyone who looks at a woman lustfully has already committed adultery with her in his heart. If your right eye causes you to sin, gouge it out and throw it away. It is better for you to lose one part of your body than for your whole body to be thrown into hell" (Matt. 5:27,28). When masturbation leads to uncontrolled fantasy, God calls it sin.

Often people who struggle with an overactive fantasy life are people reading pornographic literature, watching X-rated movies and constantly placing themselves in a position to be aroused by sexually stimulating material. I believe pornographic material will help lead anyone down the wrong path. I am convinced that those who have a problem with their fantasies should stay away from any pornographic material. Their fantasy problem, even if it does not disappear completely, will definitely be easier to control.

One more thing. If you are filled with negative guilt feelings and a real sense of insecurity, don't suffer in silence. Although it is a difficult subject to discuss, share your feelings and questions with someone you can trust. Your feelings might be well founded, but, on the other hand, they might simply be false guilt.

The Not-So-Negative Factors

I'm afraid that too many times well-meaning parents, friends, teachers and ministers have added coals to the fire when they tell kids, "If you do it, you will become sterile, blind, mentally ill or homosexual." Those suggestions contain no truth whatsoever. Whatever else can be said about masturbation, most doctors, scientists, psychologists and ministers now agree that it will not harm you biologically. Let me repeat an earlier statement: If you've had the experience you are normal; if you haven't, you are also normal.

Dr. Herbert J. Miles, in his excellent little book *Sexual Understanding Before Marriage*, makes a case for a limited program of masturbation for young men who, biologically, are at the peak of their sexual drives. For young men at this point of their lives, "we feel that a rigid condemnation of all masturbation as being sinful is rather arbitrary, unrealistic and out of harmony with the creative plan of God."[3] Dr. Miles goes on to emphasize the necessity for sexual self-control before marriage. He argues that a young man "must never violate another person to meet his sexual needs. He must lean on nocturnal emission (wet dreams) and sublimation and he may, when needed, supplement them with a temporary, limited program of masturbation."[4]

One statistic to consider is the positive trend in today's American society toward getting married at a later age. I say it is a positive trend because most teenage marriages do not make it. But because people are waiting longer, their sexual adrenaline must also wait longer. It seems to me that a limited amount of masturbation will relieve the sexual tension and not do the harm people once thought it would. My own feeling is that we've made too big an issue of this subject. We've produced too much guilt, and we have seldom mentioned the subject except in a negative way.

To be perfectly honest, as a Christian, I wish the Bible gave us a clear answer. It does not. The Bible simply does not discuss this issue. As much as I would like to give you "the answer," I cannot. There isn't one. This is a subject you will have to work through alone or with the help of someone you trust. The book of James gives some solid advice: "If any of you lacks wisdom, he should ask God, who gives generously to all without finding fault, and it will be given to him" (Jas. 1:5). Let God help you make a decision that is glorifying to Him. Remember, He created you—and your sexual identity!

* THINGS TO THINK ABOUT *

- Why do you think people are so silent about masturbation?
- If someone has a problem with masturbation, who could that person go to for a serious, confidential conversation?
- Jim mentioned the words "uncontrolled fantasy." How can that be a negative factor?
- Do you believe Jim was right or wrong to discuss the topic of masturbation with the high school guys at the camp? Do you think adults should talk openly with teenagers about sex and related matters?

* RESPECT BUILDERS *

1. Based on this chapter and other input you may have received on this subject, develop your opinion on the subject of masturbation. What are the arguments in favor of and against masturbation? In what context can masturbation be a problem?
2. Where do you stand on the issue? Because the Bible does not make a clear statement about masturbation, it may be possible that it is not a matter of crucial importance to God. Consider, for instance, the attention the Bible gives to idolatry, murder, premarital sex and gossip! God does, however, want you to be a useful, growing Christian, and anything that keeps you from being such a person is to be avoided. So if masturbation is keeping you from growing in Him, you might need to do something about it. Make sure you decide for yourself what you should do. Base your decision on prayer and on what you know about the Lord and His will for you life.

* TEAM EFFORT *

In this chapter, three views are given about masturbation: Dr. Miles's, Dr. Shedd's and Dave Wilkerson's. Of these three views, do you think any one of them is more in line with the general principles of Scripture than the other? Talk about the pros and cons of each view.

DR. MILES	DR. SHEDD	DAVE WILKERSON

AIDS

Jerry Arterburn grew up in a small Texas town. He had two older brothers and great parents, and all of them were active in their local Southern Baptist church. As Jerry grew older, he seriously considered going into the ministry. He had preached a few sermons and had been a leader in his youth group. One day Jerry had a homosexual experience. It wasn't something he had planned on having. He had been involved with girlfriends, but, nevertheless, it happened. Eventually, Jerry decided to take up the homosexual lifestyle. He suffered a large amount of guilt as he lived a life of constant partying, barhopping and promiscuity. His life grew more and more unhappy. He finally came to his senses and sought the faith of his childhood. Jerry had the courage to leave his life of promiscuity and sin and return to the Lord. He found a girlfriend. Things were going great for Jerry.

At first, when he started getting sick so often, he assumed it was a bad virus. Doctors couldn't determine what was wrong. Then came the pronouncement that must be on the mind of everyone who has ever practiced homosexuality or had a sexually promiscuous, heterosexual lifestyle. Jerry Arterburn had contracted AIDS. It's true, Jerry had come back to the Lord and changed his way of living, but the AIDS virus had been dormant in his body since his homosexual days. Jerry struggled with AIDS for several years. His strong Christian faith and the love of his family and friends kept him tough to the end, but AIDS kills, and Jerry was no exception. His funeral was a mixture of joy because of his relationship with God and sorrow that Jerry was another victim of this terrible disease.[1]

The Basics of AIDS

AIDS is caused by a virus that attacks and eventually destroys the human immune system. The word "AIDS" combines the letters of each of the four words that make up the scientific name of the disease:

Acquired **I**mmune **D**eficiency **S**yndrome

Acquired means that a person gets the disease during his or her life. In the case of AIDS, most teenagers who acquire the disease do so by sexual involvement.

Immune means that AIDS attacks the human immune system. Your immune system is your body's defense against diseases such as infections and cancers.

Deficiency means that AIDS destroys or generally weakens the immune system. When enough damage is done, a person no longer has the ability to fight off other diseases and dies.

Syndrome is a medical term that refers to a group of medical symptoms.

The AIDS virus enters the body in two main ways: through intimate sexual contact or through intravenous drug abuse. About 70 percent of AIDS cases come from intimate sexual contact, and approximately 20 percent of AIDS cases are related to using a needle to inject drugs directly into the body.

Although most AIDS carriers are homosexual, the statistics are changing. Two things seem to be necessary for a person infected with the AIDS virus to transmit the virus to a healthy person. First, the person who has the virus must transfer a body fluid that contains the virus to the healthy person. The AIDS virus has been found in blood, sexual body fluids and saliva. Second, the body fluid carrying the AIDS virus must *enter* the body of the healthy person. This can happen through a cut, a small scrape or a mucous membrane. Basically, authorities tell us that intimate sexual contact with a partner who has the AIDS virus is, and will continue to be, the main way of "catching" the AIDS virus.

Although the percentages are low, the AIDS virus can also be transmitted in a few other ways. A mother who has AIDS in her blood can infect her unborn baby. Also, a small number of medical workers have been infected with AIDS by "needle sticks." This happens when workers accidentally jab themselves with needles that contain the blood of an AIDS patient. Finally, blood transfusions with AIDS-infected blood, so far, account for approximately 3 percent of all AIDS cases.

The reason I take the time to explain some of the basics of AIDS is because many students do not have the straight facts. Either they underestimate the risk with an it-will-never-happen-to-me attitude or they are running scared with the misconception that you can get AIDS from swimming pools or public toilets.

Be Informed About AIDS

Remember, to avoid getting AIDS—*avoid intimate sexual contact.*

Today, probably the greatest risk of getting the AIDS virus comes from having sex before marriage. Not everyone who has sex before marriage will get AIDS, but, obviously, the more sexual contact a person has, the greater the chance of getting it. In some classrooms today, you will hear about "safe sex." To put it bluntly, there is no such thing. The fact is that "safe sex" practices often do not protect a person. These practices fail for many reasons. One, the person may not do everything exactly right at the right times when it comes to protection. Alcohol or drugs might affect judgment and cause a person to make mistakes. There may be failures beyond a person's control. No birth control device is 100 percent fail-safe in protecting a person from the AIDS virus.

Whenever you hear someone talk about "safe sex," think of the following example. If you were to take a revolver and put a bullet in one of its six chambers, then point the gun at your head and pull the trigger, it would be "safer" than if you had filled five of the six chambers with bullets. The risk is less. But you can hardly call it "safe." The safest thing to do is—*don't do it at all.*

Before this chapter ends, we must deal again with the issue of drugs. One of the easiest ways to get AIDS is to inject yourself with drugs by using a "dirty" needle. Drug users often share needles. Someone else's blood may remain on the needle, and you may just inject that person's infected blood into your body.

The other problem with drugs, and alcohol, too, is that your judgment is seriously affected. You may do some "stupid" things when you are drunk or loaded. One mistake is enough. With AIDS, once is all it takes.

* THiNGS To THiNK ABoUT *

- Why is it important to get the straight facts on AIDS?
- If a person chooses sexual abstinence before marriage, how possible is it to get AIDS?
- Why do you suppose a chapter on AIDS would include a message on drugs and drinking?
- What can Christians do for people who have AIDS?

* RESPECT BUiLDERS *

1. If you have ever had sexual contact or used a needle for drugs, get a test for AIDS immediately. The earlier the AIDS virus is found, the more can be done. Some people have chosen an earlier death because of the embarrassment of getting tested for AIDS. If you've had sexual contact or used a needle for drugs, you can get tested anonymously. You do not need parental knowledge to get the test.

2. Volunteer to help AIDS victims. Obviously, people suffering from AIDS are very needy. This is a time to show them the love of God. Many excellent organizations need volunteers to read, visit, run errands and share resources with AIDS victims. Check with your pastor or youth worker to find out what you can do in your community.

* TEAM EFFORT *

AIDS: A curse or natural consequence?

Divide into two groups and debate the issue of AIDS by discussing the following statements:

1. AIDS is a curse from God, *or* AIDS is a natural consequence of our fallen world.
2. AIDS victims should not be allowed to live in public, *or* AIDS victims should receive all the freedoms of anyone else.
3. A doctor who has AIDS should quit his or her medical practice immediately, *or* A doctor who has AIDS has the same rights as any other doctor.
4. A teacher who has AIDS should quit teaching students, *or* A teacher who has AIDS may continue to teach as long as he or she is healthy.
5. Homosexuality is a worse sin than adultery or fornication, *or* Homosexuality is no different from adultery or fornication.

VENEREAL DISEASE

When it comes to the subject of venereal disease, most of us try to forget that it exists. "Venereal" refers to something related to or transmitted by sexual intercourse. "Venereal disease" is any one of several diseases contracted mainly through sexual intercourse. Each year, more than 3 million cases of venereal disease are reported in the United States. Gonorrhea now ranks second only to the common cold among communicable diseases. And because more people are having casual sex these days, the spread of "sexually transmitted diseases" is at an epidemic level, according to the American Medical Association. I believe, therefore, that it is important for every person, sexually active or not, to understand venereal disease, the symptoms, the consequences and the treatments.

Gonorrhea

Gonorrhea is the most common of venereal diseases. Basically, the only way to get the disease is through sexual contact. One dangerous feature of gonorrhea has earned it the name the "silent disease": sometimes a person who has contracted it shows no major symptoms. A person may go for years without knowing he or she has the disease. In the meantime, serious physical damage may occur.

Usually, however, there are symptoms. Two to seven days after contact with someone who has gonorrhea, a woman might have a vaginal discharge, maybe mild pain upon urination and perhaps an abnormal menstrual period. A man's symptoms usually include a painful, burning sensation when he urinates and an uncomfortable discharge from the penis.

There is a cure for gonorrhea. Penicillin can cure the disease if it is found in the first stages. Without treatment, however, a person can become sterile (unable to produce children) because of damage to the sperm ducts or the fallopian tubes.

Gonorrhea has also been known to cause arthritis, meningitis and heart disease. Another sad effect of gonorrhea is that it can cause blindness in an innocent baby at birth. These are not scare tactics about venereal disease—these are medical facts!

Syphilis

Syphilis is a dangerous disease. Among communicable diseases, it is a major killer. If not treated in the first or second stages, syphilis can cause infections that will affect the heart, the brain and the spinal cord, causing serious deterioration of the body.

Syphilis, basically, consists of three stages. The first symptom usually appears between 10 and 90 days after contact. Usually a painless canker sore will appear on the penis or in or near the vagina. The canker sore will disappear after a few weeks. The second stage, which usually occurs between two and six months after contact, manifests itself as a rash all over the body and possibly a few sores on the sex organs. Tragically, by the time the disease reaches the third stage (often 15 to 25 years after it has been contracted), it is difficult to treat. It can invade the nervous system, cause paralysis and result in insanity. Blindness, swollen joints and crippling can also come in the advanced stages of syphilis.

Genital Herpes

Today, one of the most talked about forms of venereal disease is herpes simplex II. Perhaps you have read about the outbreak of herpes in our country. Genital herpes is causing some sexually active people to at least be more selective about their partners because at this time there is no known cure for herpes.

Within three weeks of sexual contact with a partner infected by herpes, a person will develop blisters around the genitals. They may experience painful urination, fatigue, and swelling in the groin areas. The blisters will pop after a few days, leaving a discharge; then the symptoms will go away. This does not mean the symptoms won't come back. Periodically, the blisters and some of the other signs will appear, often without pain. The medical profession is desperately trying to find a cure, but so far all they have is treatment that may reduce pain and help prevent secondary infection.

As you can see, and contrary to what you may have heard, venereal disease is serious business. If you have even the slightest symptoms of a venereal disease, go immediately to a physician. Yes, it is embarrassing, but these diseases cannot be "wished" away. Today in the United States, for every reported case of venereal disease, there are thought to be two or three unreported cases. Perhaps some of those people do not recognize the signs, but many of them are simply afraid to report their symptoms. They wish and hope the signs will go away and thus risk suffering major physical consequences.

In today's society, it is easy to be sexually promiscuous. Some people are in such desperate need of attention that they will go from one bed partner to another. Considering that venereal diseases are at epidemic levels, these people are playing with fire that literally can be deadly.

A young married man named Jim talked with a nurse named Arvis Olsen and asked for the latest information on cures for herpes II. Mrs. Olsen recorded this conversation in her excellent book *Sexuality: Guidelines for Teenagers.* Read Jim's comments carefully and look at the negative consequences he and his wife suffered.

> Jim came to me and asked for the latest information on cures for Herpes II. "I got this pesky disease during college and have never been able to get rid of it. Every few months I get blisters, then they disappear, only to return again later. I wasn't too worried about it until my wife's last visit to her doctor for her yearly checkup. He says she has to have a repeat on her Pap smear because the first test showed cell changes on her cervix. He told her that cervical cancers could be caused by the Herpes virus, and he also told her she would be wise not to have any more children. We have only one child, Nurse, and I'm scared to death—let me add that all this has not done a lot for our marriage. If only I had known the consequences of the 'fooling around' I did when I was nineteen! Marge and I could have the happiest marriage in the world, except...Those moments of pleasure were foolish, and the payment is unrelenting."[1]

Most people do not want to think about venereal disease, and they especially do not want to think that it could happen to them. Yet, statistics tell us that venereal disease continues to exist on an epidemic level. It won't go away just because people wish it to. Furthermore, sexually active young people today need to know the facts about venereal disease because the odds are in favor of a sexually active young person contracting this disease. One young friend of mine who contracted gonorrhea said to me, "It never entered my mind that I would get the disease. I thought it only happened to bad people. I don't think the sexual contact was worth the pain or humiliation." Remember, venereal disease is no respecter of persons.

* THiNGS To THiNK ABoUT *

- Do you think students are informed enough about venereal diseases?
- Do kids at school ever talk about venereal diseases?
- What is your opinion of "casual sex"?
- Do you think that because there is no cure for genital herpes some people will refrain from casual sex?

* RESPECT BUILDERS *

1. Venereal diseases are generally brought on from casual sexual contact. Make a commitment today to *never* have casual sex. Casual sex is against God's standards, and considering the increase in venereal diseases and AIDS, it is far too dangerous to experience a moment of pleasure and a lifetime of sorrow.
2. List several reasons to refrain from sexual contact before marriage.

* TEAM EFFORT *

Venereal Disease: An unfortunate but natural part of a fallen world, or God's curse?
For discussion:

Some people think venereal disease is an unfortunate but natural part of our fallen world. Others think it is a punishment given by God to those who dare to be sexually promiscuous. They point to the occasional upsurge of a "new" form of venereal disease as an indication of the validity of their argument. How do you feel about this issue? List reasons for and against each view.

NATURAL PART OF A FALLEN WORLD (Reasons for and against)	GOD'S CURSE (Reasons for and against)

HoMoSEXuALiTY

When Mike came into our youth group several years ago, the group loved and accepted him immediately. It was easy to like him: He was fun loving, outgoing, athletic and intelligent, and he had a real desire to grow in his newfound Christian faith. I wonder how the kids would have accepted him if they had known, as I did, that he was homosexual. I would cringe at times when some of the other kids in the group would tell "queer" jokes or would pretend to act feminine by holding a limp wrist in the air to get laughs. I would often catch myself stealing a quick glance at Mike. He never let on around the guys that it bothered him, but he sure let me know.

Mike and I would talk and talk about his feelings about being gay and being Christian—which poses a good question: Can a person be a homosexual and a Christian at the same time? I believe all sexual immorality is sin. Heterosexuals who are having sex and not married are just as sinful as is a homosexual. Although the Bible calls the homosexual act a sin, in the same passage it lists envy, deceit and gossip as sinful as the homosexual act (see Rom. 1:26-32).

Any discussion of homosexuality is complicated. But let's begin with the fact that all homosexuals are loved by God. He might not be pleased with the *act* of homosexuality, but He definitely loves the homosexual. All Christians should love homosexuals unconditionally, not for what they do or don't do, but for who they are. They are loved by our Lord just as much as heterosexuals are.

Who Is the Homosexual?

Many young people are confused about this subject, and one reason is that they may have had one homosexual experience and they think they might be gay. Many, perhaps most, young people do have what one might call a homosexual experience. Children, for instance, are curious and "play doctor" or engage in other kinds of experimentation. If this has happened to you, it does not mean you are a homosexual. It means that you, like millions of others before you, have had a normal childhood experience. Even if you as a teenager have had a few homosexual experiences, this does not mean you are gay. A homosexual person is a person who has had continued sexual activity with others of the same sex and/or is primarily attracted to those of the same sex. The person attracted to both sexes is called a bisexual.

What Causes Homosexuality?

All information is not in yet. Some experts believe homosexuality is genetic in origin. Others suggest that it comes from a hormonal imbalance. Some researchers believe very strongly that homosexuality is caused by a negative home environment, perhaps an overly dominant mother or a poor role model for a father. The best answer is that no one really knows exactly what causes homosexuality, and I'm sure the answer is probably a combination of some or all of the factors I've mentioned.

One thing is clear. If you are a homosexual, it is not necessarily your fault, but I like what Tim Stafford of Campus Life says. He writes, "The condition has been given to you. You're accountable for how you respond."[1]

Many homosexuals blame other forces for their behavior. I understand their logic and I hurt for them, but I agree with Stafford. The homosexual has the final responsibility for his or her sexual behavior. I have met people who will probably have homosexual tendencies all their lives. They may be like alcoholics—once an alcoholic, always an alcoholic, even if they never indulge. Many Christians who do have a tendency toward homosexuality have, however, chosen to refrain from homosexual actions. The sin is in the actions, not the "tendency."

Most heterosexuals do not understand what it is like to be a homosexual. They view with repugnance the actions of practicing homosexuals. As Christians, however, we must take the biblical stance of unconditional love for homosexuals. I believe, too, that it is important for us to understand this problem because within our culture we will increasingly come into contact with people who are confused about their sexuality.

Homosexuals Need Counsel

If you think you might be a homosexual, seek counsel. The longer you wait, the harder it is to understand your sexual identity. Meet with a counselor you trust and share with him or her your inner thoughts. You are not a freak! Many people share your confusion. Another piece of advice. When you are confused and hurting, don't drink or take drugs. Many sexually confused people go to the bottle, pills or marijuana to "overcome the problem." This "solution" doesn't work; it usually causes more problems.

Having encouraged you to seek counseling, I want to say one other important thing. If you want to change, I believe you can. First, it takes a strong desire to change. Second, you need God's supernatural power in your life to give you the extra support you need. Get involved in a church, read the Bible and pray daily. Third, find a wise counselor who will listen to you, care about you and hold you accountable to your resolution to change. It is also important to leave your friends who have had a negative influence on you and find a new set of friends who will be positive influences. Find friends who enjoy life and challenge you to be all that God desires you to be. I strongly recommend that you get involved with Christian friends and become active in a church.

A Story of Hope

Let me close with a story of hope. Carl was a 16-year-old who, though very shy, was a consistent participant in my youth group. One day while on a camping trip, he confided to me that he thought he was gay. He had been involved in various "gay" relationships for two years, yet he felt very unfulfilled and guilt ridden. He wanted to change, but felt chained to his gay lifestyle. He asked if I could help.

Because Carl had a strong desire to change, I affirmed his desire and got him involved in some good counseling. For support, I went with him to his first appointment. Although the counseling was somewhat painful for Carl, it was also life changing. He moved to another area of our state, but continued in counseling and became active in his new church. Today, Carl is married and has a little child. He says, "God used the counseling, the strong support from Christian friends and my church to free me from my bondage."

* THINGS TO THINK ABOUT *

- Do you believe it is a sin to be a homosexual? Why or why not?
- What would you do if one of your friends confided in you that he or she is a homosexual?
- Can you be a Christian and a homosexual?
- Do you think it is okay to make fun of homosexuals? Why or why not?

* RESPECT BUILDERS *

1. Make a decision today to never make fun of gay people. You may even be repulsed by the idea of homosexual relationships, but you will never help a homosexual change with jokes, put-downs or lack of love.
2. If you have a friend who is gay, try to convince him or her to meet with a Christian counselor who can help deal with the issues. If you encourage someone to seek help and that person receives the help that is needed, then you have been used by God in a great way.

CHAPTER TWENTY-ONE

* TEAM EFFORT *

A Case Study: John

John is one of your best friends. He doesn't seem abnormal at all. He likes cars, sports and has been active in the church youth group with you. One night on a back-packing trip, you and John have a serious conversation. John tells you he thinks he is gay. He shares with you that he has had two homosexual experiences with an older neighbor and now he is really confused. He doesn't know if he is homosexual, or heterosexual. He asks for your advice and friendship. As a group, talk about what you would say and do.

PORNOGRAPHY

Cliff is a popular, outgoing senior in his church and school. Cliff has more friends than anyone I know and he has two great parents. *Cliff is addicted to pornography.* It all started innocently enough. Cliff was spending the night with one of his best friends. His friend showed Cliff his stash of his father's old "girlie magazines." Cliff looked at each picture and had a rush of excitement such as he had seldom experienced. His mind continued to put those pictures back in his brain for weeks. Cliff daydreamed about the pictures often at school, and a few weeks later, he stole one of those kinds of magazines from a local market. His zeal for pornography continued throughout junior high and high school. His language was a little coarse, he had been involved sexually with a couple of girls, and yet he still remained active in his youth group. He told me later, "I felt like I was living a double life. I wanted to be a good Christian. My quiet secret was that hardly a week went by without me viewing something pornographic."

What started as an innocent look at *Playboy* magazine turned into a craving for bizarre sexual pornography. He moved from what is called "soft-core" pornography to "hard-core" pornography. What finally scared him was the realization that he actually got sort of "high" from watching child pornography (which is when children are engaged in sexual activity with adults or other children).

On the outside, Cliff looked like a regular Christian guy. On the inside, he was living a dual life. Cliff finally concluded that he needed help. Today, with the aid of a counselor, his family, friends and God, he is breaking the strong addiction of pornography.

Is Cliff's story that unusual? No, I'm afraid not:

- Ninety-nine out of every 100 guys have looked at pornographic materials.
- Nine out of 10 girls answer yes to viewing pornography.

Some studies tell us that 50 percent of the American teenage population view something pornographic each and every month. Wow! If you are not careful, pornography can get a hold of you very seductively and not let your mind forget the pictures you have placed there.

It's a fact that most people are drawn by curiosity to seek out a pornographic magazine or movie. Yet, just because a person has read a dirty magazine or seen a dirty movie doesn't make him or her a pervert. Continued and constant obsession with pornographic material, however, can be dangerous.

When speaking on the subject of tortures, sex perversions and murders, former Detroit, Michigan, police inspector Herbert Case said, "There has not been a sex murder in the history of our department in which the killer was not an avid reader of lewd magazines."[1]

Phoenix, Arizona, Police Chief Paul E. Bluebaum said, "Our city has experienced many crimes of sexual deviation such as child molestation and indecent exposure. We find that most of these deviates read obscene material and often exhibit them to the children in an effort to arouse sexual excitement among their victims."[2]

Pornography is a cheap substitute for sexuality as God created it to be. It often treats a human as a sex object. Pornography makes people feel dirty and uneasy about their sexuality. Our sexuality is a gift from God. Sexuality is definitely not the perverted and often quite obscene thing it is portrayed as in so many books and magazines.

The Effects of Pornography

Many students have gone far deeper into pornography than they ever imagined. Some people haven't actually realized how negative the effects of their bad habits really are. Authorities give us several negative results of viewing pornographic material. I want to key in on two of the most common effects for teenagers.

A Warped View of Sexuality
People who frequently look at pornography begin to view sex as nothing but lust. Every element of love is replaced with a degrading and harmful view of sexuality. Far too often, in the words of Dr. Jerry Kirk, "pornography exploits and dehumanizes women and children as discardable tools for the satisfaction of male lust, and children are abused mentally, emotionally, physically and spiritually to satisfy the hedonistic urges of pedophiles (child molesters). Women and children, when molested and cast aside, are left with indelible scars for the rest of their lives."[3]

People involved in pornography begin to tolerate and trivialize ungodly sexual behavior. I believe it is absolutely impossible to put a steady diet of pornography into your mind and expect to have a healthy Christian view of sexuality. Exposure to pornography makes people much more likely to believe that the greatest sexual joy comes *without* the commitment of marriage.

Guilt and Shame

When Cliff talked to me about his obsession with pornography, he was filled with the emotions of intense guilt and shame. He was beginning to isolate himself and draw away from his family, church and friends. I'm convinced if Cliff would have continued much longer in his lifestyle and addiction of pornography, he would no longer have felt guilty. The Bible says that eventually these people, "Having lost all sensitivity," will give themselves over "to sensuality so as to indulge in every kind of impurity, with a continual lust for more" (Eph. 4:19).

Let's get something straight. Pornography is very dangerous. We cannot take this subject lightly. The power of a pornographic picture is all-consuming. Dr. Jerry Kirk gives us several important facts about pornography:

1. Pornography destroys the image of God in people. After all, we are created in God's image.
2. Pornography is addictive. "Pornography subtly winds around its users an ever-tightening chain of bondage."
3. Pornography is anti-Christian. Pornography openly mocks the most precious Christian beliefs. It belittles issues such as marital fidelity, morality and commitment to Christ. Here's what the Scripture says, Do not be deceived: Neither the sexually immoral nor idolaters...will inherit the kingdom of God....The body is not meant for sexual immorality, but for the Lord, and the Lord for the body (1 Cor. 6:9-13).
4. Pornography is antisex. "Pornography promotes physical satisfaction without caring love, sex without responsibility, union without obligation for the consequences and exercise of the mating privilege with no regard to the immediate personal and physical consequences or the eternal consequences originally designated by God to accompany it."[4]

If you have been experimenting with pornography, I hope this chapter has sobered you to the facts and consequences of this lifestyle. Today is the day to stop the habit of viewing pornography. Similar to a recovering alcoholic who is unable to even take a sip of wine without going back to a life of alcoholism, you must decide to stop all behavior centered around pornography. Note the following steps:

Step One: *Today, make a commitment to God to never view another raunchy magazine or movie again.*

Ask God to clean these memories from your mind and create a clean heart. The good news is that God is more powerful than pornography. He can and will forgive you of your sins and cleanse you from unrighteousness (see 1 John 1:9).

Step Two: *If you have talked to God and still feel drawn toward this addictive habit, seek help immediately.*

You are not alone. Thousands of well-meaning people in this world are addicted to pornography. Seek out a pastor, counselor or trusted friend who will listen to you and help you develop a plan to overcome this chain of bondage around your life. Cliff needed to talk to a trusted Christian counselor. That counselor is helping him learn to live one day at a time and remove any perverted sexuality from his life. With the help of God and his counselor, Cliff will overcome this obstacle.

Step Three: *Your mind matters.*

When we talk about pornography, we must talk about our minds. I like to use the old phrase "garbage in, garbage out." The principle is simple: If you put garbage into your mind, eventually garbage comes out. The more garbage you put into your mind, the more garbage there is to come out in the form of all kinds of negative behavior. The best way to keep away from a negative thought life and negative behavior is to deprive your mind of garbage. Feed your mind good things—and good things will come out. Feed your mind trash—and guess what comes out? Paul offers some good advice about our thought lives: "Finally, brothers, whatever is true, whatever is noble, whatever is right, whatever is pure, whatever is lovely, whatever is admirable—if anything is excellent or praiseworthy—*think* about such things" (Phil. 4:8, italics added).

Dr. James Dobson calls the battle against pornography "the winnable war." The war can be won when we guard our hearts and minds by not allowing pornography to enter into our lives. Please do not underestimate the power of pornography. Run from it and run toward the love of God. He is the Creator of positive, healthy sexuality. Everything else is a counterfeit.

* THINGS TO THINK ABOUT *

- Given the strong message of this chapter, what are your reactions?
- What do you think about the statement that pornography can be addictive?
- Why do you suppose our culture allows such blatant pornographic material to reach the hands, eyes and minds of young people so easily?
- What are several practical ways to keep away from pornography?

* RESPECT BUILDERS *

1. Your mind matters. Read Philippians 4:8. List the various kinds of things it suggests you think about—whatever is true, noble and so on. Then, beside each of those words, write one or more things that fit into that category. The first two are done as an example for you. Fill in more of your own ideas for those two and then continue with the remaining words. Discuss your findings with your group or family.

THINK ABOUT SUCH THINGS THAT ARE...	THINGS THAT FIT THE CATEGORY
True	God's Word is true.
Noble	My grandparents are noble people.

2. Search the Scriptures for thoughts on pornography. Read each verse or passage and then put in your own words how this section of Scripture might relate to pornography.

1 Corinthians 6:9-13	
Ephesians 4:18,19	
Ephesians 5:11	
Colossians 3:5-14	
Philippians 4:8	

SEXUAL ABUSE

The following question was handed to me recently while I was speaking to a group of junior high and senior high students: "After someone has been sexually abused and hasn't told anyone about it and it has gone on for about five years, how can I try to forget and deal with it?" I receive such questions all the time. I never like to hear these questions. Yet, after several years of experience I now realize some important issues need to be thought about and questions need to be answered about sexual abuse. Did you know that:

- One out of 4 young women will be sexually abused by age 18, and
- one out of 8 young men will be sexually abused by age 18?

Diane was 12 when she told me that her grandfather had been "messing around" with her since she was 5 years old. Diane and her sisters had all been sexually abused by their grandfather.

Steve is 31 years old, but he still vividly remembers the exact evening a baby-sitter molested him. He was only 8 years old.

Janet had never been more excited. Bob finally asked her out on a date. She had dreamed of this night for almost two years. They got something to eat at a local hamburger stand and then went on to a party. Bob and Janet started drinking wine coolers. Both were feeling "pretty good" from the alcohol buzz when Bob said, "Let's go for a drive." They parked and started kissing. Bob's hands began to wander. Janet felt uncomfortable, but didn't say anything. They were going too far. She was extremely nervous and very frightened. She said, "Stop!" He kept on going. Janet tried to get away. He got rough; Janet cried and screamed. Janet's dream night turned into a date rape.

These are not pretty stories. These are not happy statistics. Unfortunately, the statistics have names and faces. These people are friends I know, but I guarantee that you also know people who have struggled with the trauma of sexual abuse. You, too, may be a person who has been victimized by this tragedy we call "abuse"

Most people want to forget about this horrible experience. They pray it will go away, but it doesn't. When someone has been sexually abused, that person's pain tends to run deep and affects every aspect of life.

Here's what I generally tell students who have been abused:

1. *It's not your fault.*
   It's always the fault of the abuser. Sexual abuse is a horrible crime against you. The abuser is sick. If you blame yourself, you will get sick also.

2. *Seek help. Don't suffer in silence.*
   Most people who have been abused sexually are afraid to tell anyone. However, you can't get better without help. Your pain won't go away by itself. You simply can't wish it away. I urge people who have been abused to not wait another day but to seek help immediately. If you wait, it only gets more difficult. It doesn't get easier.

3. *There is hope!*
   Unfortunately, thousands have been abused. Many people have sought help, however, worked through their pain and are now living happy lives. Many people who have been abused believe that life will never be happy again. I can understand that their emotions are paralyzed; however, the truth is that there is hope.

4. *God cares!*
   Frankly, most people who have experienced any kind of sexual abuse struggle in their relationships with God. I can understand their hurts and confusion. But I'm afraid too many people spend their energies blaming God instead of being comforted by Him. God wants to walk with you through the valley of hurt and disappointment. God weeps at your tragedy. He loves you and wants to heal your wounds.

This is a difficult chapter to write, and I struggle with the idea of including it. It seems, however, that no one today is exempt from the harsh reality that tragic experiences happen to both good and bad people. If you or a friend of yours has faced some of the difficult experiences mentioned in this chapter, seek outside help. This chapter does not provide all-inclusive information. It is written as an overview and as a catalyst for action.

Date Rape

Date rape is a rape by someone you know or are dating. Frankly, most women who are raped are raped by someone they know and trust. Familiarity is enough to make them let down their guard, sometimes enough to make them wonder afterward whether they were really raped. A major myth about rape is that rapists are always strangers. Most rapes are committed by acquaintances. In fact, 75 percent to 80 percent of all teenage rapes are acquaintance or date rapes. If you have been date raped, immediately talk to someone who can help you. Although a date rape may not always result in a serious physical injury, it almost always causes severe emotional distress. You can receive help when you talk with a trusted counselor, pastor or teacher.

Rape

As much as we all wish our society was always safe, it's not. Today, as never before, we must take precautions to prevent violent rape.

Rape is perhaps the ultimate outrage. Rape is one of the most horrible crimes committed against a person of the opposite sex. Rape is most often inflicted not as a *sexual* crime, but as a *violent* crime. Most rapists are not so much interested in sexual pleasure as in hurting and frightening the victim. There is usually a great deal of anger, aggression and hatred within the psychological makeup of the rapist. Most victims of rapes are women and girls, although in the last few years an increase in the number of homosexual rapes of men and boys has been occurring. In this chapter, for convenience, I will refer to rape victims as women.

A person who has been raped should immediately call the police or go to a nearby hospital or rape crisis center. She will usually meet understanding people and will be checked for injuries. The victim should not wash up before going to the hospital or center. A doctor will check for and collect evidence of the rape. Almost all the people, from doctors and nurses to police officers, are caring individuals who will compassionately help the rape victim through her initial shock and pain.

A rape victim should not go through this process alone. She should get the best medical treatment available along with some professional counseling. Receiving help from many trained individuals can and will make recovery from this painful experience a little easier.

Even better than coping with rape is preventing it. The very best protection is to stay away from potentially dangerous situations. Too many people have not thought through their actions and have lived to regret it. Here are a few suggestions to help prevent a rape. I encourage you to get in touch with your local rape prevention or crisis center for more information.

- Never hitchhike. You're asking for trouble.
- Don't walk or jog alone at night. This can be dangerous.
- Carry a whistle. Put the whistle on your key chain and keep it in your hand when you are alone.
- Don't go out alone with a person you don't know. Too many people have been "picked up" at a dance, amusement park or other public place without

realizing they were being picked up by a rapist.

- Don't flirt with someone you don't know. You could be flirting with a rapist

Here are some important facts about rape:

- In the United States, a rape is reported approximately once every six minutes.
- Rape is one of the most frequent violent crimes, and its incidence is steadily increasing.
- Victims range in age from small children to the elderly. They come from all lifestyles and socioeconomic groups.
- Rape is a crime of violence. The rapist uses force or threats of harm to overpower and control the victim.
- Although rape may or may not result in serious physical injuries, it almost always causes severe emotional distress.[1]

Incest

Incest is having sexual relations with a member of your own family, and sadly, incest is far more common than most people imagine. The most common form of incest is a father-daughter relationship, but many cases are reported each year of sexual relations between mother and son or brother and sister as well as between other relatives.

Incest is a serious and sensitive subject because it deals with family members. There is no such thing as a positive experience involving incest. An incestuous relationship must be stopped. If you or someone you know has been involved with incest, do not keep it to yourself. Report it to a proper authority immediately. A good place to start would be a minister, social worker, counselor or police officer. The victim of incest will need help and so will the aggressor. Sometimes victims of incest believe the experience is their own fault. Such faulty thought patterns produce extreme but completely unnecessary guilt and self-blame. The victim of incest is not at fault and should not take the blame for someone else's sickness. Furthermore, no one is doing the aggressor a favor by keeping quiet about the problem.

At age 16, Linda confided in me that she had been forced into an incestuous relationship with her father from the time she was 7 until she was 13. I never would have guessed her problem in a million years. On the outside, she appeared to have it all together, but on the inside, she lived with tremendous amounts of hurt, anger, bitterness and guilt. By the time she saw me, she was a volcano ready to explode at any minute.

Here are the steps I went through with Linda. First, as her youth pastor, it was important for me to be a support and encouragement to her. She needed someone to lean on, so my wife and I both became good listeners for her. Second, we felt she needed extensive counseling and so we referred her to an experienced psychologist and trusted friend. We let him deal with the major psychological trauma and we continued as supportive friends and pastors. The Christian psychologist reported the crime of incest to the county, and the family was able to go through intensive counseling.

At the right time, a biblical counselor made contact with Linda's father and found he was open to counseling. Over the next two years, we watched a broken relationship mend. Scars, and at times resentment, are still present, but Linda has blossomed into a beautiful young woman both inside and outside. On her wedding day, she was able to allow her father to walk her down the aisle.

Having worked through a difficult situation, Linda now says she would not have been able to do it without God's help and the healing and loving support of friends. Linda actually came to the point where she forgave her father before he died, which wasn't easy. But some people are not as fortunate as Linda was. They may never be able to forgive their aggressors. In situations involving incest, no one should expect instant forgiveness or instant healing of broken relationships. It may require a long time for the victim to reach the point of forgiving the aggressor. Still, I believe all people who have experienced the devastation of incest should seek help. There *is* hope—just ask Linda.

* THINGS TO THINK ABOUT *

- Why do you suppose the statistics for sexual abuse are getting higher and higher?
- To whom would you go if you were abused in any way?
- Why are people afraid to tell anyone about their abuse?
- What role should God play in the life of a person who has been abused?

* RESPECT BUILDERS *

1. If a friend has been sexually abused, assist that person in seeking help immediately. The person needs professional care. You can be the catalyst for a positive life-changing decision.
2. Become aware of some of the signs of sexual abuse. Your friends may express their pain through behavior rather than words. The following is a list of several signals of sexual abuse, although the mere fact that a teenager has one or more of these behaviors does not always mean he or she has been sexually abused.
   a. Learning problems in school;
   b. Poor peer relationships;
   c. Self-destructive behavior, suicidal tendencies, frequent drug and alcohol abuse;
   d. Hostility and lack of trust toward adults;

e. Major problems with authority figures;
f. Seductive, promiscuous behavior;
g. Running away;
h. Fear of going home, fear of being left alone with the abuser;
i. Severe depression;
j. Pain, itching, bleeding and bruises in the genital areas;
k. Extremely low self-image.

If you suspect an incestuous relationship, consider these potential signals for abusive sexual behavior on the part of adults:

a. Demands isolation of the child—discourages friendships, school activities and dates;
b. Enforces restrictive control—allows few social events (actually extremely jealous);
c. Displays overdependence—sometimes the parent will depend on the child to fill needs usually met by the spouse or other adult;
d. Indulges in frequent drinking.[2]

* TEAM EFFORT *

A Case Study: Sexual Harassment and Abuse

Bonnie was baby-sitting at her ex-boyfriend Tom's house. She was close to his little sister and his family although she and Tom had broken up. Tom's stepfather had always been nice to Bonnie. In fact, she often wished she had a father as special as Tom's stepfather.

Tom's family was going out to dinner and a play while Bonnie watched the youngest child. Tom's stepfather, Ted, would be home, but he would be working in the back room.

The moment Bonnie put the little girl to bed, Ted came into the kitchen and asked Bonnie if she wanted some popcorn. Bonnie loved popcorn and said, "Thanks, that will be a good addition to the program I'm watching on television." Ted made the popcorn and then sat down on the couch next to Bonnie and started watching the program with her. Bonnie complained about a sore back she had gotten from playing softball. So he began to rub her back. At first he rubbed outside her sweater, but after a while moved his hands under her sweater.

Bonnie froze. She didn't know what to do. She didn't know if this nice man was going to go farther or if he was just doing an innocent favor. Bonnie was tense and nervous. In a soft voice, he told her to relax; it would be better for her backache.

The phone rang. Bonnie was grateful for the distraction. Ted, reluctantly it seemed, got up to answer the phone.

1. If you were Bonnie what would you do?
2. Do you think it was okay to baby-sit while the stepfather was still home? Why or why not?
3. If you were Bonnie's youth pastor and she told you this story, what would you say or do?
4. If you were Bonnie, would you tell Tom or his mother about this incident? Why or why not?

QUESTIONS AND ANSWERS

In the past 20 years, I've had the privilege of speaking to thousands and thousands of teenagers and of hearing them talk about their sexuality. Everywhere I go, I appreciate their openness, honesty and sincerity in asking important questions. In this chapter, I have selected some of the questions that have been asked most often. My biggest problem was keeping it to only 16 questions!

1. Is lust a sin? How can I handle my fantasy life?

Jesus made a strong statement about lust in the Sermon on the Mount. He told His followers, "You have heard that it was said, 'Do not commit adultery.' But I tell you that anyone who looks at a woman lustfully has already committed adultery with her in his heart" (Matt. 5:27,28). I'm sure the reason Jesus called lust a sin is that He knew the important part the human mind plays in life. The place to overcome temptation is in your mind. Believe it or not, your mind is your most important sex organ. I'm sure that at times everyone has a strong sexual imagination and that at times lust barges into everyone's mind. The question is what to do with it when it arrives.

The following are a few brief suggestions for controlling lust and your fantasy life

- Be assured that you are normal. Nearly everyone you know will have those kinds of thoughts occasionally.
- Don't *feed* your thought life with pornographic magazines, books, films, music, jokes and so on. I believe a person can starve his or her fantasy life and cause many of the negative thoughts to go away.
- If you feel completely consumed by lust in your mind, seek the wisdom of a trusted counselor.
- Seek God's help in delivering you from your problem. God is interested in

every aspect of your life. Talk to Him about your problems, ask Him for insight and deliverance, and then be open to His answers.

- When you catch your mind beginning to wander, immediately replace those unhealthy thoughts with positive thoughts. Paul gives good advice in Philippians 4:8: "Whatever is true, whatever is noble, whatever is right, whatever is pure, whatever is lovely, whatever is admirable—if anything is excellent or praiseworthy—think about such things."

2. Is oral sex wrong? What is your opinion of having oral sex instead of intercourse before marriage?

I get asked this sort of question at every seminar I teach on sexuality! My personal opinion is that oral sex is not necessarily wrong in marriage. I believe that if both marriage partners consent and if their sexual exploration is not physically abusive, then it isn't wrong. But when it comes to premarital oral sex, I have a different opinion. I think couples who engage in oral sex are playing with fire. Some couples say it is a form of birth control! I really don't see how couples can keep from having intercourse if they are experiencing oral sex. The emotional and physical intimacy involved in oral sex, however, is far too similar to intercourse. If your boyfriend or girlfriend gives you the line that oral sex is great and you'll get all the same feelings without intercourse, don't buy that line. Too many people try to make a major distinction between sexual intercourse and oral sex, but the emotions and degree of intimacy are far too similar to clearly separate the two experiences.

3. Is it possible for sperm to go through my clothing and get inside the vagina?

The common word for this kind of sexual activity is "mutual masturbation." Usually the male is stimulated to ejaculation while rubbing his penis against the female's genitals while one or the other or both still have on their clothes. Many young people practice mutual masturbation as an alternative to the real thing. I think people must be careful to avoid this form of sexual activity. First of all, although it can create a wonderful feeling for the male, the female is usually not as stimulated by this experience. It's very one-sided. Second, mutual masturbation can create negative habits that can carry on into marriage. Premature ejaculation, for instance, is a problem in marriages and is often the result of poor premarital sex habits. Third, mutual masturbation can lead to the real thing. Once you've experienced the "imitation," it's easier to desire the real thing. Fourth, to respond directly to the question, there is a slight chance, depending on the specific garments, that sperm can swim through clothing. But it is not very likely to happen.

4. Should we get married just because we are having intercourse?

The answer is no, no, a thousand times no! I've met too many couples (including Christians) in marriage counseling sessions who have told me the major reason they got married was that they were having premarital sexual intercourse and they believed it was best to get married instead of continuing to sin. Couples should never get married only to make their sexual intercourse "legal" in God's eyes. That is simply silly, and too many times the marriage ends in disaster. The odds are that if you start a marriage for the wrong reasons, the foundation will crumble and nothing will be left to rebuild the marriage.

Sometimes a guy or girl will try to force the other person into marriage because the two are having intercourse. One will try to press guilt on the other. It's true that premarital intercourse is wrong, but two wrongs definitely don't make a right. The best way, then, to tell whether you are getting married for the right reason is to quit having sexual intercourse and see if your desire to marry each other remains as strong as it was.

5. Are you still a virgin if you had intercourse at age seven but didn't really know what it was? I thought it was a game.

I believe you are still a virgin. Many young people have innocent sexual encounters when they are really too young to understand much about their sexuality. But the majority of people need not feel weird or strange about such an occurrence. Most sexual exploration at a young age is innocent. If this experience constantly bothers you, then I suggest you seek counseling. If this experience was what you could define as sexual abuse (see chapter 23 for more information), however, then you should definitely seek help.

6. How young is too young to get married?

I don't think there is any magical age when marriage becomes right! Because you asked, however, I'll give you a straight answer: most teenage marriages fail. It may be true that in our parents' day more teenage marriages seemed to work, but the odds are very much against a teenage marriage working today. Most teenagers do not have the emotional, mental and spiritual maturity to commit their lives to another person in marriage. They are still growing and changing. One couple I know that was married when they were both 17 told me that by the time they were 22 they had changed so much that they didn't have enough in common to stay married. Yet they were in a heap of trouble because now they had two small children—Tanya, age two, and Kenny, age four—to think about. A divorce would affect all four of them. Now whatever decision they made would involve four people instead of only two.

If you are totally convinced that you must marry as a teenager, make sure you go through extensive marriage counseling. If you won't do this, I question your maturity. Remember, too, that most teenage marriages fail. I can think of exceptions, but they are not the norm. When I was a teenager, I thought I was mature enough to handle major responsibilities. Now I realize that even though I *thought* I was smart enough to handle something like marriage, I really wasn't. It's a good thing I didn't get married then. I was far too young and immature to be making such a major, lifelong and life-changing decision.

7. Is it true that once a guy gets the best of you he's no longer interested?

I understand your phrase "gets the best of you," but I sure don't like the wording. If a guy is only trying to "get the best of you," then he was never interested in the real you in the first place. But to answer your question, I'm afraid it is sad but true that some guys do lose respect for and interest in the girl after she has "given in." The girl who "gives in" is taking a major chance that her special friend will lose interest in her. I honestly think that if a girl or guy says "no, let's wait" and true love is involved, the other person will respect that stand and will be willing to wait. I personally would rather be safe than sorry.

8. Do guys really want to marry a virgin?

I think most people would love to marry a virgin. The idea of two people giving one another the special gift of their bodies for the first time in marriage is beautiful and right. All you have to do, however, is look at the statistics to see that perhaps 75 percent of first marriages are not between two virgins. One or both partners have had a previous relationship or have had premarital intercourse together. Because this is true, it means that as Christians we are called to forgive and to love unconditionally. Just because a person has had sexual intercourse before you met him or her does not necessarily mean he or she will not be a good marriage partner.

9. What is your opinion of sexually promiscuous teenagers using birth-control methods?

First, let me emphatically state that I believe sexual intercourse is only for married couples. The best "birth control" is God's way—sexual abstinence before marriage. I'm very concerned about the apparent freedom of medical clinics handing out birth control pills and condoms with what I call value-neutral sex education.

Birth control is a tough issue. Some people would think that by including the question in this book I am condoning birth control and teaching young people to "sin safely." I don't think I am. Although it is not an easy issue, I believe if you are considering having sexual intercourse, or have had sexual intercourse and are choosing not to obey God, you should talk to someone you love and trust about birth control. If I must be pressed on the issue, I would say that if you choose to do wrong, then for the sake of the potential baby use birth control to prevent any more heartache than you may already be causing by your actions. I like Charlie Shedd's advice. He calls it "Two Truths for Unmarried Teenagers About to Have Sex":

1. That boy who has intercourse without taking precautions is too irresponsible to deserve the name "father."
2 That girl who has intercourse without taking precautions is too irresponsible to deserve the name "mother."[1]

Of course, the best and right answer about teenage birth control is to choose God's way, which is sexual abstinence before marriage.

10. How often do married people usually have sexual intercourse?

Great question. I always wondered about that when I was in high school, too. It's not as though most of us feel comfortable asking Mom or Dad that question!

Statistics show that some married couples have intercourse once a month and some have intercourse almost every day. Ray Short, a sociologist, writes that the average number of times a week is three and that the number of minutes for each experience, including foreplay and "afterglow," is eight.[2] The average grand total of sexual activity in a given week would be 24 minutes! As you can see, a relationship that is primarily based on sex isn't much of a foundation for a positive relationship.

11. What is an orgasm?

An orgasm or climax is the peak of excitement in sexual activity. For a male, the orgasm takes place when the semen is ejaculated from the penis. A female orgasm is a rush of good feelings accompanying a series of vaginal contractions. The contractions may vary in number and in intensity for different people and at different times.

12. What is sadism? What is masochism?

Sadism is a mixture of sex and violence. A sadist is a person who gets a kind of sexual pleasure from hurting someone or inflicting pain. Sadism is a sickness, a mental disorder. Keep away from anyone you think might be suffering from this disease. Masochism is another disorder in which a person needs to endure pain and abuse to experience sexual pleasure or satisfaction.

13. What are the differences between an older guy and a younger teenage girl? Is it safe to date a guy who is seven years older than I am?

The answer, of course, depends on the maturity of the individuals involved. Some 17-year-old girls or guys are very mature for their ages, and some 24-year-olds still act like 13-year-olds. It's my opinion that most of the time a dating relationship between an older guy and a teenage girl doesn't work. I also think some important questions need to be considered regarding this kind of relationship. Ask yourself, for instance, why would an *adult* seven years older than I am be interested in me? Is it primarily a sexual interest? Is he more serious about the relationship than I am? Will I miss out on some of the fun of high school by dating an adult? What have his past relationships been like?

Even asking this question shows you have some real smarts! I hope you will take a long, slow, rational look at the pros and cons of the relationship and then seek the advice of people you love and trust. Ask a variety of people. Ask people your age. Ask your parents, youth workers, teachers and anyone else who might have an opinion you trust. My answer would usually be that I highly question if it would be the best thing for you in the long run to date an adult who is seven years your senior. Life is too valuable and short to take many chances when it comes to adult/teenage relationships.

14. Will I suffer any adverse psychological effects if I don't have a boyfriend until college? (It's not my choice! I'd like to have a boyfriend now!)

This is one of the all-time great questions. I appreciate your openness and honesty. I surely do not believe that anyone should or will suffer "adverse psychological effects" because of lack of dating life in high school. If such effects existed, up to 50 percent of the people in high school would be in big trouble!

I can imagine how hard it must be to really desire to have a boyfriend (or girlfriend) and yet never have that kind of relationship, especially when others are beginning to date. But take heart. Many people never date in high school and others never date in college. I call them "late bloomers." Some of these late bloomers end up having the greatest times in high school and college because they aren't tied down—though they would not have minded a date or two or one hundred! It is hard not to be asked to homecoming or the big dance, but, unfortunately, everyone doesn't get asked.

My advice is don't spend your time waiting for that phone call! Keep busy, keep active—and I'm 100 percent convinced that eventually you'll have a special relationship that will make all the waiting worth it. The worst thing you can do is sulk and retreat from others. This will only cause deep hurt and resentment. I know a number of girls and guys who didn't date in high school and who now have wonderful relationships with those of the opposite sex. I bet you'll have the same thing happen to you.

15. Is marijuana dangerous?

I've heard it said for years that marijuana is only a weed, not a drug. It has been said that this weed is basically harmless and it shouldn't be a big deal to smoke a few joints once in a while. That is simply misinformation, especially in the 1990s. Research tells us that the marijuana used today is 10 to 20 times stronger than that available a decade ago.[3]

Researchers today are also concerned that chronic marijuana use might cause permanent damage to the reproductive system as well as various emotional problems. Is marijuana dangerous? For some, a joint once in while may never affect them. For others, that joint could be the beginning of a tragedy. I, for one, am not willing to take the chance.

16. What is AIDS?

At the time of this writing, we are experiencing one of the most frightening diseases in the entire history of our world. The Acquired Immune Deficiency Syndrome, more commonly known as AIDS, is racing throughout the world and killing people at epidemic proportions. Research says that "right now African doctors estimate that as much as 7 percent of the entire population of both Zaire and Tanzania are infected with the fatal disease"![4]

The majority of AIDS victims are male homosexuals, along with some intravenous drug abusers. At the present time, however, many victims do not fit these categories. AIDS attacks the body's immune system. The mode of transmission seems to be primarily through sexual contact with body secretions, through tainted hypodermic needles and through blood transfusions. Those particularly vulnerable will be those who engage in promiscuous sex. My suggestion is to learn all you can about this disease. Little is known about AIDS, and what you might hear could be rumor or speculation. Be sure to read about AIDS in chapter 19.

A FRANK DISCUSSION WITH PARENTS AND YOUTH WORKERS

Experts tell us that only about 10 percent of students today receive good, positive, healthy Christian sex education. Did you? Probably not. Considering some of the outstanding material on sexuality available to churches today, it's sad to say the church is still not doing the best job either. It's unfortunate that parents and the church have remained more or less silent when it comes to healthy sex education. Sexuality isn't an easy subject to discuss with our kids, but I believe our silence is really hurting this generation of young people who desire to hear the truth.

I speak to more than 100,000 students a year on this subject alone and I'm still shocked by the statistics:

- Twelve million teens are sexually active. Eight out of 10 males and 7 out of 10 females report having had intercourse when they were in their teens.
- If present trends continue, 40 percent of today's 14-year-old girls will be pregnant at least once before age 20.
- By age 20, 81 percent of today's unmarried males and 67 percent of today's unmarried females have had sexual intercourse.
- Fifty percent of all sexually active 19-year-old males had their first sexual experience between the ages of 11 and 13. Among nonvirgins, 50 percent of the

boys and 18 percent of the girls first had intercourse at age 18 or younger.[1] Seventy-four percent of teenagers say they would live with someone before marriage or instead of marriage.

Keeping these statistics in mind, how can we as parents and youth workers still remain silent? If you are like me, these statistics frighten you, yet we all know they are probably true. We are raising a generation of teenagers who are trying to imitate sexually active adults but who still make decisions based on teenage emotions. I hope we as adults can be more open and understanding when it comes to helping our young people deal with their sexuality.

All kids are curious when it comes to sex. Sex is mysterious and our kids, like ourselves at their age, have a real curiosity and hunger to find out more about their bodies and about sexuality. I think it is a shame that so much of a young person's sex education must take place in the locker room, by reading *Playboy*, through the media or even in the value-neutral sex education of some public school systems.

Be Open

It's time to open up! It's time to talk about sexuality with our kids. They don't understand it much better than you did at their age, and, yet, they are probably more sexually involved than any generation before them. After I talked with a group of parents recently about teenage sexuality, a parent challenged me by saying, "I'm not sure we should talk to our children about sex. The more information they get, the more curious they become. The more curious they become, the more apt they will be to indulge."

Good thought, but completely wrong. Many young people today do not have the slightest idea how important or sacred their sexuality is. They've bought our culture's lie, "If it feels good, do it." They've never had the privilege of an explanation of what their sexuality is all about. *They need you.* Our young people need you to share with them in an open, honest way about sexuality. They need you to sit with them and really communicate the hows and whys of their sexuality. Remember, the more positive, healthy, values-centered sex education kids receive, the *less* promiscuous they will become.

One young person told me recently, "My dad told me not to do it, but he never told me why not to do it and when I did it, I was disappointed. I wish he had explained his opinion to me." When it comes to sexuality, I believe firmly that young people who have had an open, honest relationship with their parents and/or youth workers have much healthier attitudes and will find themselves in less trouble in the long run.

Teach Biblical Sexuality

Biblical sexuality is much more than "God says not to do it!" Biblical sexuality teaches that God created our sexuality—and not only did He create it but He sees it as very good (see Gen. 1:31)!

Too many Christian and non-Christian kids today think that God hates sex. As I've said before, they think He's the great killjoy in the sky. Often they have these thoughts because no one has ever taken the time to share with them about sex from God's perspective.

We need to communicate to our kids that our bodies and our sexuality are gifts from God (see 1 Cor. 6:19,20). These gifts should be respected and taken care of. We must teach the biblical view that intercourse before marriage is called sin. Then, keeping in mind the statistics quoted earlier in this chapter, we must make sure our kids learn about grace and forgiveness. I'm afraid most kids are illiterate when it comes to sexuality and the Scriptures. You have the rare privilege of giving them the insight they desperately desire to have.

Talk About Related Subjects

Believe it or not, your kids want to know your opinion on subjects relating to sexuality. They want to know your thoughts on peer pressure, abortion, dating, unconditional love, the pill and so on. All of these subjects and others are being talked about at school, and both youth workers and parents must deal with these subjects to balance some of the misinformation kids are getting from so-called "experts"— their peers who are making up the story as they go along. I'm afraid that often our kids don't listen to us because we always want to give them *the* answer without ever listening to them. Although the kids may be dead wrong, we need to listen to them. Listening is the language of love. When I let kids share their views, they are more open to other views. Sometimes they've never heard other perspectives or verbalized their own views, and when this happens, the kids often will change their minds!

Teaching Methods

Sexuality can be discussed with young people in many ways. The particular method we use is not as important as the fact that we find time to have those open and honest discussions about these important issues. Here are a few ideas to help you develop a more open and honest relationship for talking about sexuality.

Films: Visit a library, a Christian film distributor or a videotape rental source. Use both Christian and secular films as springboards for discussion.

Books: Read a book together. Good material on sexuality and related subjects is available.

Newspapers: Nearly every day the newspaper includes articles that can serve as discussion starters.

Classes: Take a human sexuality class together. Many schools offer special courses on sexuality. Take the class with your kids and use the lessons as springboards for continued discussions. Be sure to look into what the course will cover. Some of the human sexuality courses offered are "wild and crazy" and can be offensive to your belief system.

Youth Group Activities: Youth workers can use many other valuable learning methods. Case studies can be used effectively, as can questions written out anonymously and answered by the youth workers or parents. Some groups use panel discussions and have good results. Many youth workers today will bring in an expert to speak with their groups. You can usually find a youth worker, doctor, nurse, teacher or psychologist in your area who will do an excellent job of leading a seminar.

The point I'm trying to make in this chapter, and in this book, is that kids need parents and youth workers to use every method available to teach about one of the most important subjects to all of us—our sexuality.

Keep an open mind, be willing to share your feelings, be open to disagreement, be sensitive to needs—and everyone involved will become a better person. By discussing sexuality with your young people, you may prevent some negative experiences. You will also be giving the gift of a healthful attitude and godly stewardship of one of God's most special gifts to us—our sexuality.

GLOSSARY OF TERMS

The definitions in this section are provided for your convenience. The words listed are largely restricted to terms used in this book. For help with words not on this list, see a dictionary.

Abortion: The premature ending of a pregnancy. Two kinds of abortion are known. *Induced abortion* is a medical procedure performed at the request of the woman or her doctor. *Spontaneous abortion*, also called "miscarriage," is a natural termination usually because of some problem in the development of the fetus.

Abstinence: The voluntary avoidance of something, as in the voluntary avoidance of sexual intercourse.

Adoption: The act of taking a person into one's family and raising him or her as one's own child. Unwed mothers sometimes allow their babies to be adopted by others.

Adultery: Voluntary sexual intercourse between a married person and a partner who is not the husband or wife.

Arousal: Excitement, stimulation.

Birth control: *See* Contraception.

Bisexual: Pertaining to both sexes; having both male and female sexual organs; sexually attracted to members of both sexes.

Cervix: The narrow, lower part of the uterus.

Climax: *See* Orgasm.

Clitoris: The small, sensitive organ at the upper end of the vulva. It corresponds to the penis.

Conception: Impregnation. Penetration of the ovum (female egg cell) by a sperm.

Condom: *See* Contraception.

Contraception: (Birth control.) The prevention of conception by use of devices or drugs. Commonly used methods are: *Birth control pill*—A drug made of synthetic hormones that prevents ovulation. Available only by prescription; must be used exactly as prescribed. *Condom*—A thin rubber sheath placed over the erect penis before intercourse to prevent sperm from entering the vagina. *Vaginal foam, jelly, suppositories, sponge*—Nonprescription products that are applied to the inside of the vagina. Most contain a spermicide—a chemical substance that kills sperm cells. *Diaphragm*—A thin rubber shield that covers the cervix and prevents sperm from entering the uterus. Must be individually fitted by a doctor. *Premature withdrawal*—Withdrawal of the penis from the vagina before orgasm. Largely unreliable because sperm may be released before ejaculation. *Rhythm method*—Abstinence from intercourse during the woman's fertile days as determined by her menstrual cycle.

Douche: Cleansing of the vagina with a stream of liquid such as water or other substances.

Egg: *See* Ovum.

Ejaculation: The emission of semen from the penis.

Embryo: An unborn baby from the moment of conception to the beginning of the third month of development. (At this point it begins to be referred to as a fetus.)

Endocrine: A gland producing an internal secretion that regulates or controls functions of other parts of the body.

EPT: Early Pregnancy Test. Available without a prescription to determine if a girl or woman is pregnant.

Erection: The enlargement and hardening of the penis or clitoris as tissues fill with blood.

Estrogen: A hormone that promotes the menstrual cycle and affects the development of secondary sexual characteristics in the female (breast development, widened hips and so on).

Extramarital: Outside of marriage. Often used to refer to illicit sexual intercourse—"extramarital affair."

Fallopian tube: The tube through which the egg (ovum) passes from the ovary to the uterus.

Fertilization: The act of initiating biological reproduction; the penetration of the ovum by a sperm, resulting in conception.

Fetus: The unborn child from the third month after conception until birth.

Fondle: To stroke or caress with affection.

Foreplay: The first stage of a sexual experience, during which partners may kiss, caress and touch each other to achieve full sexual arousal.

Fornication: Sexual intercourse between unmarried partners.

French kiss: A kiss in which the person's tongue enters the partner's mouth.

Genital herpes: A viral disease that causes blistering of the genital areas; sexually transmitted. (*See* Venereal Disease.)

Genitalia: (Genitals, genital organs.) The reproductive organs, particularly the external, visible organs such as the clitoris, vulva and vagina in women and the penis and testicles in men.

Gonorrhea: *See* Venereal Disease.

Guilt: The fact of being responsible for an offense or wrongdoing, the remorseful awareness of having done wrong. "Real guilt" refers to the fact of having done wrong and to the   appropriate awareness of having done so. "False guilt" refers to hanging on to these guilty feelings, being unable to forgive oneself even after the offended party has extended forgiveness.

Herpes: *See* Genital Herpes.

Heterosexual: A person who is attracted to or sexually active with persons of the other sex.

Hormone: A chemical substance, produced by an endocrine gland, which has a specific effect on the function of other organs in the body.

Immoral: Contrary to accepted morality.

Incest: Sexual intercourse between close relatives such as father and daughter, mother and son, or brother and sister.

Infatuation: A short-lived and superficial attraction to another person.

Intercourse, sexual: The act whereby the penis is inserted into the vagina. (Note: The word "intercourse" alone can refer to communication, an exchange of ideas between persons or groups.)

Masochism: Cruelty to oneself; receiving sexual pleasure from experiencing pain or harsh domination.

Masturbation: Stimulation of one's own sexual organs, often to the point of orgasm.

Menstruation: The periodic discharge of blood from the uterus through the vagina.

Nocturnal emission: (Wet dream.) An involuntary occurrence of male erection and ejaculation during sleep.

Oral sex: Stimulating the partner's sexual organ with the tongue and/or mouth.

Orgasm: The peak of excitement in sexual activity, characterized by a series of muscular contractions.

Ovaries: The two female sex glands found on either side of the uterus, in which the ova (egg cells) are formed. They also produce hormones that influence female body characteristics.

Ovulation: The release of an ovum (egg) from the ovary to the fallopian tube.

Ovum: (Plural: ova.) The egg, or female reproductive cell, found in the ovary. After penetration by a male sperm, the human egg develops into an embryo and then into a fetus.

Penis: The male sex organ through which semen and urine are discharged.

Pornography: Literature, films, pictures or other means of expression that exist solely for the sake of sexual arousal and having no concern for personal or moral values.

Pregnancy: The period from contraception to birth; the condition of having an embryo or fetus within the body.

Premarital: Before marriage.

Prenatal: Before birth.

Procreation: The act of producing offspring.

Progesterone: A hormone that prepares the uterus to receive the fertilized ovum.

Promiscuous: Engaging in casual sexual relationships or in sexual intercourse with many persons.

Prophylactic: A device or drug used to prevent disease. Common term for condom.

Rhythm method: *See* Contraception.

Rape: Forcible sexual intercourse with an unconsenting partner.

Sadism: The need to inflict pain on the partner in order to receive sexual pleasure.

Semen: The fluid, containing sperm, that is ejaculated through the penis when the male reaches orgasm.

Sexual intercourse: *See* Intercourse, sexual.

Sperm: The male reproductive cells, produced in the testicles, discharged in the semen through the penis and capable of fertilizing the female egg.

Spermatic duct: (Vas deferens.) The tube in the male through which sperm passes.

Spermicide: A substance that kills sperm.

Sterilization: A procedure by which a male or female is rendered unable to produce children; he or she is still able to engage in sexual intercourse. Some common methods are: *Laparoscopy*—An operation in which small incisions are made in the abdomen, allowing the surgeon to cut or cauterize the fallopian tubes. *Tubal ligation*—An operation in which the surgeon cuts and ties the ends of both fallopian tubes. *Vasectomy*—An operation in which the male sperm-carrying duct is cut and tied.

Sublimate: To modify the natural expression of an impulse, such as sexual desire, in a socially acceptable manner.

Syphilis: *See* Venereal disease.

Testicles: The two sex glands in the male that secrete sperm.

Tubal ligation: *See* Sterilization.

Uterus: The muscular, pear-shape female organ in which the fetus develops.

Vagina: (Birth canal.) The passage in the female body between the uterus and the vulva. It receives the penis during intercourse and is the canal through which an infant passes at birth.

Vasectomy: *See* Sterilization.

Venereal Disease: (VD.) Any of a variety of contagious diseases transmitted almost exclusively by sexual intercourse. Some of the most common are genital herpes, gonorrhea and syphilis.

Virgin: A person who has never had sexual intercourse.

Vulva: The external genital organs of the female.

Wet dream: *See* Nocturnal emission.

Womb: *See* Uterus.

NOTES

Chapter 2
1. Larry Richards, *How Far Can I Go?* (Grand Rapids: Zondervan Publishing House, 1979), p. 96.
2. Ibid., p. 43.

Chapter 3
1. C. S. Lewis, *The Screwtape Letters* (New York: Macmillan Publishing Company, Inc., 1982), p. 83.
2. Ray E. Short, *Sex, Love or Infatuation: How Can I Really Know?* (Minneapolis: Augsburg Publishing House, 1978), p. 83.
3. Ibid., pp. 83, 88-89.
4. Richards, *How Far Can I Go?* p. 43.

Chapter 4
1. *Focus on the Family* magazine (April 1990).

Chapter 6
1. Bill Ameiss and Jane Graves, *Lord of My Life, Lord of Me* (St. Louis: Concordia Publishing House, 1982), p. 75.
2. Jane Norman and Myron Harris, M.D., *The Private Life of the American Teenager* (New York: Rawson Wade Publishers, Inc., 1981), p. 54.
3. Ibid., p. 42.

Chapter 7
1. Josh McDowell and Paul Lewis, *Givers, Takers and Other Kinds of Lovers* (Wheaton, Ill.: Tyndale House Publishers, 1980), p. 89.

Chapter 10
1. Aaron Haas, *Teenager Sexuality: A Survey of Teenage Sexual Behavior* (Los Angeles: Pinnacle Books, 1981), pp. 46-49.
2. Ibid.

Chapter 12
1. Scott Kirby, *Dating: Guidelines from the Bible* (Grand Rapids: Baker Book House, 1979), p. 49.
2. Ibid., p. 51.

Chapter 14
1. Charlie Shedd, *The Stork Is Dead* (Dallas: Word Inc., 1968), p. 83.
2. For a more in-depth look at this subject, you may want to see Steve Arterburn and Jim Burns, *Drugproof Your Kids* (Ventura, Calif.: Regal Books, revised edition, 1995), the audiocassette of "Drug Proof Your Kids" (Colorado Springs: Focus on the Family, 1989), or the video *Drugproof Your Kids* (Ventura, Calif.: Gospel Light, 1995) for parents and youth workers.

3. Steve Arterburn and Jim Burns, *Drugproof Your Kids* (Ventura, Calif.: Regal Books, revised edition, 1995), pp. 175-177, used in part.

Chapter 15
1. James Dobson, *Emotions: Can You Trust Them?* (Ventura, Calif.: Gospel Light, 1980), p. 18.
2. Jim Burns, "The Guilt Glob," *Sprint* (Elgin, Ill.: David C. Cook Junior High Curriculum), pp. 1-2.

Chapter 16
1. Shedd, *The Stork Is Dead*, pp. 61-63.

Chapter 17
1. Focus on the Family, *The First Nine Months* (New York: Dell Publishing Co., Inc., 1990), p. 3.

Chapter 18
1. David Wilkerson, *This Is Loving?* (Ventura, Calif.: Gospel Light, 1972), p. 40.
2. Shedd, *The Stork Is Dead*, p. 72.
3. Herbert Miles, *Sexual Understanding Before Marriage* (Grand Rapids: Zondervan Publishing House, 1975), p. 146.
4. Ibid., p. 147.

Chapter 19
1. For a complete story of Jerry Arterburn, his fight with AIDS and his faith, read Jerry Arterburn with Steve Arterburn, *How Will I Tell My Mother?* (Nashville: Oliver Nelson, 1988).

Chapter 20
1. Arvis J. Olsen, *Sexuality: Guidelines for Teenagers* (Grand Rapids: Baker Book House, 1981), pp. 63-64.

Chapter 21
1. Tim Stafford, *A Love Story: Questions and Answers on Sex* (Grand Rapids: Zondervan Publishing House, 1977), p. 103.

Chapter 22
1. Wilkerson, *This Is Loving?*, p. 40.
2. Ibid.
3. Dr. Jerry R. Kirk, *What the Bible Says: Ten Reasons Why You Should Get Involved in the Fight Against Pornography* (Colorado Springs: Focus on the Family, 1989), p. 5.
4. Ibid.

Chapter 23
1. Jim Burns, *The Youth Builder* (Eugene, Oreg.: Harvest House Publishers, 1988), p. 279.
2. Ibid.

Chapter 24
1. Shedd, *The Stork is Dead*, p. 76.
2. Short, *Sex, Love, or Infatuation*, p. 54.
3. Rana Rottenberg, "The Care Medic: Answering Questions About Marijuana Use" (Orange, Calif.: Care Unit Hospital of Orange, 1980), p. 1.
4. William H. McIlany, "AIDS: Is Time Running Out for Treatment?" *Orange County Business Journal* (1985): 8.

Chapter 25
1. Jim Burns, *Surviving Adolescence* (Dallas: Word, Inc., 1990), p. 84.

Books and Resources from Jim Burns